£8

W.C.

from

D.W.S.

for

a Happy Birthday

11 . 2 . 47

" THE STREET "

LET'S WALK DOWN FLEET STREET

BY

C. W. SHEPHERD

GERALD G. SWAN

LONDON

First published 1947 *by*
*Gerald G. Swan Ltd., Edgware House, Burne Street, N.W.*1

THIS BOOK IS PRODUCED IN
COMPLETE CONFORMITY WITH THE
AUTHORIZED ECONOMY STANDARDS

MADE AND PRINTED IN GREAT BRITAIN BY
ALABASTER, PASSMORE & SONS, LTD., LONDON AND MAIDSTONE

CONTENTS

LIST OF ILLUSTRATIONS

Foreword

THIS book is more a biography of Fleet Street than an auto-biography of the author, less an account of Fleet Street at work than at play. Indeed the title—and heaven knows, I considered many before deciding on the present one—might have been " The Lighter Side of Fleet Street," except that I should never have forgiven myself for choosing it.

" Come, sir, let us take a walk down Fleet Street," Dr. Samuel Johnson is credited with saying, but the most careful combing of Boswell fails to reveal the old boy as saying anything of the kind ; while Walter G. Bell, in his " Seven Centuries of Fleet Street," quotes George Augustus Sala as admitting that it was he who set the saying on its Johnsonian way, as a mild practical joke. Be that as it may, it explains my choice of a title.

One of the best known streets in the world, " ours " is always something of a mystery to those not engaged in it. " How interesting to work in Fleet Street! " people say, and they are right. In this book I have tried to tell the uninitiated a little about this companionable place—this Street of Adventure, this Street of Ink, this Street of No Sleep, as it has been called in turn. No description of it, however, is so apt as that which has called it a village.

A village it is, a community wherein newspapermen know each other with all the intimacy of a small country town, where gossip, repartee—and even scandal—flow with the fluidity of Fleet Street's own ink, where social life is self-contained, and where, as in a village, the " outsider " is regarded with slight reserve, even though he come from no farther than the West End.

That the book contains omissions I am well aware, especially where the " big shots " are concerned. How, it may be asked, could one omit stories of the youthful Arthur Christiansen, regally paid *Daily Express* Editor, known only as " Chris," even by those who speak that friendly name with bated breath—an editor who, like the brilliant Frank Owen, until the war, editor of the *Evening Standard*, and his predecessor, Percy Cudlipp has debunked the idea that great editors must not " mix " in Fleet Street ?

You may wonder, also, why the newspaper barons—the Rothermeres, the Beaverbrooks and the rest—find no place in it. The reason is simply that this is not a book about " big shots," but men whose work makes the backcloth of the daily drama of newspaper production, so far as its editorial side is concerned.

Written by a newspaperman, about newspapermen, and illustrated by Fleet Street men and no other, I hope it will be conceded that it is a real book of " The Street," differing in many ways from any which have gone before it.

My thanks for the drawings go to Will Farrow, Edward Swann, Tom Cottrell, " Glossop," Sidney Potts, Ted Davison, George (" Tommy ") Thompson, and to Gilbert Rumbold for his fine and comprehensive picture of " The Street " itself. All have been done exclusively for this book.

Also I must pay tribute to Jack McCail for the brisk and pleasing jacket which, with true artist's forgetfulness, he has omitted to sign.

Let's Walk Down Fleet Street

CHAPTER I

This Way to Fleet Street

LONDON is the only city in the world which has a street of newspapers. Fleet Street, that short, comparatively narrow thoroughfare linking the Strand with Ludgate Circus, harbours every kind of publication that ever had ink put into it. The *Methodist Recorder* casts a doubting eye towards the *News of the World*, and *Blighty* was a neighbour of the *Daily Telegraph*. The London Offices of provincial newspapers huddle together as closely as mice on a cold night, and the day comes and the night follows it, yet rarely do you see a newspaper door closed in this street of no sleep.

It is a hard street for those who work in it. It has killed many, de-ambitioned more, and made the fortunes of quite a few. It has been blessed and blasted by the public in turns. It has received—perhaps sharing it with the medical profession—more criticism than any calling save phoney herbalism. It has distorted news ; it has ground axes ; reputations have been damned by it, inaccuracy fed at its poisonous breast, and it has, in general, been about as much good to the country as the wrath of God. These, at least, are the views of thousands who would raise hell if they did not have their paper in the morning.

I have nothing to say to such, except that it would do them good to spend a day and night in a newspaper office and see the journal start from zero, see the news come pouring in from every quarter at home and abroad, and see the sifting of it and the indefatigable checking of it, see the writing, re-writing, condensing and captioning of it—all to present in the morning that miracle called a newspaper.

> " Within your wholesome and convenient field
>   The truest miracle is daily done.
> Never forget that men have tamed and taught
>   The lightning ; clad it in a livery known
>   As news."

Fleet Street runs due east and west, and, because of this, provides at times two of the most beautiful prospects in London. You have only to stand half-way down it at sunset to see what I mean.   The sun, sinking behind the Strand, casts its rays straight down the street, tipping its irregular buildings with opal gleams.   At the western end stands the lantern tower of St. Dunstan's, which, with the reddening sun streaming through its filigree, gives definite point to the word " lantern."   Look east and there, at the top of Ludgate Hill, looms the dome of St. Paul's through the evening haze.   At times the sun catches only the golden cross surmounting it, turning it into a living symbol.

It was on such an evening, as I stood watching it, that a man spoke to me. I knew him well as a newspaperman who had been broken on Fleet Street's inky wheel, and whose days were now declining. I had never suspected him of looking deeply into anything save a pint pot. Yet out he came with this :

" You know, Shep, when that view is as it is to-night, it always reminds me of ' Abide With Me '—you know, in the hymn."

" In what way ? " I asked.

" Just two lines," he replied, and quoted :

> " Hold Thou Thy Cross before my closing eyes,
>   Shine through the gloom, and point me to the skies."

With which he turned into the " Cheshire Cheese " for what he called a little joy-water.

Fleet Street is not short of " joy-water." Pubs glisten in and about it like jewels in a crown. The Punch Tavern, Old Bell, White Swan, Auntie's, Kings and Keys, Falstaff, Ye Olde Cheshire Cheese and the Old Cock Tavern. These are some of them ; but not all. No wonder the newcomer meets grief when he unthinkingly accepts a challenge to do the rounds and have a drink in each. No wonder, also, that a temperance reformer once described our short street as the " Devil's Furlong." There was, by the way, a pub in Fleet Street long ago called the " Devil

Tavern," and a plaque marks its site. A chapter on taverns will be found later in this book.

The heterogeneous architecture of Fleet Street gives it much of its charm. There is the great *Daily Express* building of black glass, utterly modern and incomprehensible in its curves, whilst, quite near it, is the massive *Daily Telegraph* office of grey granite, carrying an eastern touch which prompted someone to liken it to the Hanging Gardens of Babylon. These giants seem to dwarf the miscellany of other and older buildings which make up the street. A fair number of these house the London offices of provincial newspapers, such as the *Yorkshire Post*, *Birmingham Post*, *Dundee Courier* and a host of smaller ones, many under the same roof, all adding to the journalistic population.

A large proportion of Fleet Street men were " something else " before they entered journalism. In my own case, I spent my first few years as a junior resident master in a Midlands college and enjoyed every minute of it, for the school stood in a beautiful countryside, and there was plenty of time for sports, fishing and halfpenny nap in the masters' study. It was here that I extended my earlier knowledge of country things and people, with the result that I have been a fairly prolific writer about them, to say nothing of a Coronation Day country broadcast which I shall mention later on.

While here I began writing an occasional short story for the local paper, which my vanity made me read and re-read until the type danced. I am not the only one to confess this, for even the most successful writer never ceases to get a kick out of seeing his name in print.

Then an odd thing happened.

There was going to be an affair called the Pan-Anglican Congress in London, attended by bishops and big clerical guns from all over the Empire. The vicar of the village church, which we had to attend twice every Sabbath, was dead nuts on this congress, and preached about it every Sunday for weeks—as though the villagers cared ! I had never written an article, but here, I thought, was my chance to try. I therefore kept a mental note of everything the old vicar said, until I knew as much as he did about the forthcoming event. Then I wrote to a high-class monthly called the *World's Work*, offering to write an article on the subject, and, to my astonishment, they agreed. I think it must have been the college note-heading that did it, and no doubt they thought I was the headmaster, and a parson at that.

Anyhow, in it went. By chance, the issue happened to be the one containing the half-yearly index, and there, under the heading " Authors," was my name. I was an Author !

That did it, of course. It *had* to be journalism after that.

I managed to acquire a copy of the Literary Year Book which contained the names of a wide variety of newspapers, periodicals and publishers. With more industry than I have ever since displayed in correspondence, I wrote a fixed number of letters daily to newspapers, agencies, publishers and heaven knows what besides, asking for a job.

This general offensive was not very successful. I had even written to *Chambers's Journal,* and in this case I received a letter from Mr. Chambers, head of that old and distinguished firm, urging me to put journalism and its precariousness out of my mind and stick to teaching. I never see the Journal now without thinking of that kindly letter, hand-written on paper as thick as a slate.

At last I had a bite, not, perhaps, from a very big fish, but nevertheless an important one. It was the Northern Newspaper Syndicate, which had its headquarters in the grey old town of Kendal, Westmorland. I had no idea what a newspaper syndicate was, but imagined it to be a string of newspapers all in one stable. On the contrary, a syndicate, in the journalistic sense, is an agency supplying features of every description to newspapers at home and overseas.

The upshot was that I went to Kendal at the quaint salary of £90 a year. I would have gone for half that sum. In any case, you could do a great deal in a country town in those days on about 34s. a week.

One may ask—why Kendal for an important agency ? The answer is two-fold. The syndicate was started in a small way by John Watson, a Quaker, who, having discovered that he could sell his own articles simultaneously to non-conflicting papers, say *Newcastle Journal, South Wales Echo* and so on, conceived the idea of selling other people's articles in a similar way. Mr. Watson was really the pioneer of syndication. Being a Quaker, in a mainly Quaker town, he was loath to leave it, so he built up the Syndicate where it started. It was a considerable concern, with its editorial department, printing works and the rest.

The other reason was that most of the Provincial newspapers were in the north—Lancashire and Yorkshire bristle with them—so that they were easy of access, whilst the carriage on matter sent out in metal stereo was far less than it would have been from London.

My main job, apart from general writing and sub-editing, was to think out ideas for a series of articles by eminent people, and I was put into a nice little square room to do my thinking alone.

I started off with the suggestion for a series called " My First Break," and it was to include an article by the Archbishop of Canterbury entitled " My First Sermon." I took the typescript of the series down to John Watson, the Editor-in-Chief, and he could not have been more surprised had I suggested " My First Kiss " by the King.

" It's at least ambitious," I was told laconically, and the idea progressed no further than birth. However, I hung on to it and eventually produced a similar series which was used.

In between thinking out features, I did a considerable amount of general writing, and discovered that one need not be an expert to write on experts' subjects. I wrote for a time a weekly feature called " Veterinary Advice " which was syndicated to country weeklies. The feature gave me a perpetual headache, but as it perhaps saved a few cows the belly-ache, I suppose it was not in vain.

But my days with the firm were numbered, and in about six months I was out of a job. I had given up my earlier profession, had gained no particular experience of journalism, and was in a strange town which offered no possibilities in my own line. I was young. I was raw to the world, and I certainly little thought that the time would come when I should return as managing-editor of the organisation.

My problem now was what to do. I decided to stay in Kendal and devote myself to writing short stories, having already sold one or two to C. Arthur Pearson, Ltd., for the *Royal* and *Novel* magazines. I had left on quite good terms, and Mr. Watson, when he heard of my intentions, wrote advising me to go elsewhere, find a job of some kind and continue my free-lance activities " from that vantage point." This was not to my liking. My hand was already on the plough.

So I acquired a couple of semi-furnished rooms, which remained " semi " until I left them. But they certainly became the centre of such Bohemianism as existed in a Quaker town. The subdued spirits of the place had never had such an outlet as they had in my bare rooms, where hitherto isolated intellects gathered together. We knew no hours, but talked the daylight in. We also played a gambling card-game called " Farmers' Glory " and drank much beer. I suppose in a way I was sowing my wild oats, but, as G. K. Chesterton put it, they were only Quaker oats.

After a time there fell vacant at the Syndicate a post of some importance. It involved for the most part visiting Provincial editors to discuss with them their feature programmes ; that is to say, their plans for all matter except news and advertisements, the kind of matter which the Syndicate provided. It included serials and short stories by famous authors, articles by the eminent, and weekly and daily " columns " ranging from " Woman's World " to " Chess and Draughts," and from " Children's Corner " to " Chats with the Doctor." I was offered the job and gladly accepted, especially as it entailed frequent visits to London, meaning Fleet Street, for the Northern Newspaper Syndicate supplied quite a number of *non*-syndicated features to London newspapers and periodicals. With the prospects of visits to Fleet Street, I felt " like some watcher of the skies, when a new planet swims into his ken."

In time I acquired a personal knowledge of nearly every newspaper office in the country, and became familiar with cities and towns from Plymouth to Peterhead. I have since found it a happy lubricant in friendship to know a man's own town when he is far away from it. There were, by the way, some strangely named papers on my visiting list, including the *Penzance Evening Tidings*, the *Kidderminster Shuttle*, the *Redditch Indicator*, the *Leith Burghs Pilot*, the *Surrey Comet* and the *Skibbereen Eagle*.

As mentioned earlier, I had already written stories for the firm of Pearson's, and I never went to London without calling on Mr. P. W.—now Sir Percy—Everett, head of the firm, asking for a job. It became rather a joke between us.

AN IMPRESSION OF THE AUTHOR
By Ted Davison

" Still keen on getting to Pearson's ? " P.W.E. would say with his kindly grin. " I really believe you *will* one day." And that day came. I left Kendal and joined the firm at whose door I had knocked so long. I have something to say later of my days with that happy firm, but first of all let us settle the Kendal matter. I had been at Pearson's something under two years when the managing-editor of the Syndicate resigned, and the proprietor offered me the job. The salary was tempting, I liked the Lake District and had made many friends there, but, most of all, I relished the turn of events which enabled me to return as managing-editor of the firm from which I had been sacked a very few years before. I think that was what really did it !

Anyhow, I knew I should sooner or later land in Fleet Street for good, which I did in several years' time. This was when I became a director of Newspaper Features, Ltd., a young and rapidly expanding feature agency, soon to become the leading one of its kind in the country. Sir Robert Donald, late editor of the *Daily Chronicle*, and Sidney Dark were also directors, but the agency was run mainly by myself and the brothers Taylor— H. A. and G. V. The former later became President of the Institute of Journalists.

CHAPTER II

A "HAPPY SHIP"

THERE is an expression among sailors—"A happy ship." It signifies a ship wherein everybody, from cabin-boy to captain, " hits it off " with everyone else. Changes in the crew make but little difference to a " happy ship " ; it seems to keep up its reputation of its own accord.

The firm of C. Arthur Pearson, Ltd., was a " happy ship." I have never known a happier.

It was founded by C. Arthur Pearson, who later went blind and devoted the rest of his life to the welfare of St. Dunstan's. Popular education was on the move when Pearson thought he would like a journal of his own, on the lines of the recently started *Answers*, by Alfred Harmsworth, later Lord Northcliffe, and *Tit-Bits*, by George Newnes, with whom Pearson worked for a time. Later, both Pearson and Newnes became baronets. The two firms now work together as Newnes and Pearson, Ltd.

When young Pearson was looking around for money with which to start his magazine in a small way, he went to Sir William Ingram, owner of the *Illustrated London News*.

" What do you propose to call the journal ? " asked Sir William.

" Well, I thought of calling it *Pearson's Weekly*," replied the baronet-to-be.

" Good heavens ! " exclaimed Sir William. " *Pearson's Weekly* ! But nobody *knows* you."

" Quite right," said Pearson, timidly, " but they would if I called it *Pearson's Weekly*, wouldn't they ? "

He got the money.

When I joined Pearson's, Sir Arthur was dead. He had slipped while entering his bath and fatally injured himself. This left Peter Keary in control, with P. W. Everett—now Sir Percy—as his immediate colleague. Others in the " ship " were F. E. Baily, Charles Vivian, Walter Brett, Bernard Everett (P.W.E.'s brother) and William Pollock. The first four edited respectively the

Royal Magazine, *Novel Magazine*, *Smallholder* and the *Scout*. Pollock later became the brilliant cricket correspondent of the *Daily Express*, accompanying at least one Test team to Australia. At Pearson's, however, he was, like myself, a journalist of many parts—" all things by turn, and nothing long."

We were a friendly crew, one of our institutions being visiting each other's rooms in the afternoon for tea. None of the higher-ups seemed to mind, so long as we did our work; which is as it should be. I even remember P. W. Everett, who had become Chief when Peter Keary died, saying : " Oh, will you be in to-morrow, Shepherd ? " when once suggesting a job I should do. I'm sure he would not have minded had I said no. But he would have wanted the job done, all the same.

At the time of Mr. Keary's death, Bill Pollock had, as one of his jobs, the selection of prize-winning anecdotes in *Pearson's Weekly*. They came in on post-cards—hundreds of them—and payment was made for those used each week. On the day after Mr. Keary's death, Pollock came into my room, which I then shared with an elderly, seigneur-like journalist named White.

" Here's a really good one, Shep," said Pollock, handing me a postcard, " but it has a bit of the irreligious about it. Wonder if we should print it ? "

I read it, but was in two minds about it ; so we consulted White, who read it, stroked his long moustache and read it again. Then he shook his head slowly.

" No, I don't think we should use it," he said, with a misty gleam in his eye. " *It might get Mr. Keary into trouble.*"

Have you ever insured against twins ? You might have done, in those days, through the medium of *Pearson's Weekly*.

The next editorial colleague of P.W.E. was Mr. Lamburn, who had *Pearson's Weekly* under his wing. Lean, aesthetic and charming, Lamburn was the most prodigious smoker I have ever known. Always he had a two-ounce tin of navy cut before him, which I am sure was replaced almost every day. If tobacco be a steadier of nerves, Lamburn must have needed all of that when the great Twin Insurance Scheme was running.

The idea was that any woman expecting a child during the coming July could insure against their being twins by taking *Pearson's Weekly* regularly during the preceding three months and keeping the necessary coupons. If twins arrived in July, the coupons entitled the mother to £5. Five pounds was quite a nice sum for anybody in those days, to say nothing of the poorer elements of *Pearson's Weekly* readers. It seemed a good scheme, and well ahead of rival journals—all at that time vying with each other to produce circulation schemes.

Everything had been worked out actuarially. Statistics for previous Julys had been studied, and an estimate made of the number of " P.W." insured readers who would have twins. The number seemed well within the economic compass of the scheme. So far, so good.

Then came July, and with it the first applications from mothers with a plural bent. The first few were greeted with glee, the two hundredth with gloom. Something was wrong. Surely every bearer of twins could not have been a reader of *Pearson's Weekly*? Yet apparently they were, for applications came in from all sorts and conditions of mothers all over the country. Pearson's had bargained for only a small proportion of twin-bearers having signed " on the dotted line," but here they were faced with something more than that. They were faced with paying five pounds to five times as many mothers as they had anticipated.

Every morning brought still more applications from the fruitful, until somebody in the office had a brain-wave and thought of midwives. He wondered, in fact, if, owing to the elastic terms of the scheme, it might not have been possible for midwives to buy a few copies of the journal weekly, so that, should twins occur to any of their charges, they could go to the mothers and say in effect :

" Look ! *You* haven't taken *Pearson's Weekly*, but *I* have. With my coupons you can claim five pounds—fifty-fifty."

Of course, that explained everything. It meant that Pearson's might have to stand up to an indefinite number of twins—even those born in maternity homes, for nurses were no doubt as astute as midwives.

There were conferences with the firm's lawyer ; there were conferences among ourselves, but there was no conference with any Oracle who could point a way out. The nearest approach was the suggestion that we should discover the proportion of

genuine " reader-mothers " to midwives, with the idea of main-
taining that midwives' coupons were not in accordance with
the scheme.

This meant that a considerable number of claims had to be
investigated, and it was mainly the lot of the staff to investigate
them. Almost apologetically, we were given our " briefs," and
off we went.

It happened that most of my " cases " lay in the East End of
London, and I came up against the reality of poverty in a way
which shocked me. I had heard of slums, of course, in that
vague way in which so many have heard of them, but I had never
imagined the existence of such squalor. My first visit led me up
the soul-less stone stairway of a great tenement block. A vin-
dictive July heat lay upon the place. It beat upon the roof,
blazed in at the windows and seeped through the very walls at the
top of that high building. A tawdry woman—the mother—
answered my knock, and listened with widening eyes when I told
her I was from *Pearson's Weekly*.

A preliminary to our inquiries was to make sure that the twins
actually existed. I asked to see them.

" You shall see them all right," said the woman. " So you're
from the paper ? It seems too good to be true."

Opening a door, she showed me into a room, in the middle of
which was a large bed. There was a sudden buzzing sound, a
cloud of flies rose from the bed like a black lid, and there, on a
wet, grey sheet, lay the twins.

" There you are," said the woman, proudly, triumphantly.

I backed out hastily ; then listened to how Mrs. So-and-So,
the midwife, had brought her the coupons with which to claim
the money. I knew—or thought I knew—that she had no chance
of claiming it, but I did not tell her so. She would hear from
Pearson's Weekly very soon, I said.

This happened at Shadwell. My next visit was in St. George's-
in-the-East, a dockland slum. Here I found a man in charge
of the twins—a wizened, rather elderly little man. He told
me that he was a dock labourer out of work, and that his wife
had already resumed her occupation as a part-time char. I asked
to see the twins and he pointed to two converted orange boxes.

" They're in there, on the straw. The authorities provided

the boxes because we've nowhere to put them. We only live in this one room . . ."

Then he admitted that the coupons had come from the midwife, and almost tearfully " hoped it wouldn't make any difference." I told him the chances were that it would, but that I would do my best for him.

Of course, I found quite a few genuine cases, and so did my colleagues. Eventually, our reports were considered by the firm. Several of us had stressed the pathetic side of the matter, and I am sure this was not overlooked when the " happy ship " decided to pay everybody in full.

Pearson's Weekly was always to the fore among journals having competitions such as " Limericks." Big money prizes, running into hundreds of pounds, were offered in these competitions, and entries came in by the thousand. In the case of " Limericks," competitors had to devise a lively last line for a verse, of which the first four lines were given. There were also competitions which required the competitor to make an epigrammatic quip in four words based on the given example. Thus, if the example were " VERY STRANGE," a likely winning Snaplet, as one paper called them, might have been : " Butcher—' Curing ' Dead Pigs."

It was in connection with one such competition that Pearson's acquired a headache worse than the one given them by the twins. It is often asked if all entries to newspaper competitions are scrutinised, and from my experience the answer is 'Yes.' I often used to stroll into the competition room at Pearson's and watch the staff at work. They sat round a large table with a raised desk at one end at which sat the " president," the man who had the last say as to which entries should be taken to the editor for final judgment.

At intervals a clerk would place a wad of entries before each adjudicator, to be renewed when dealt with. With great conscientiousness each man would peel off the coupons, examine them with an acquired rapidity, putting aside any of special merit. The latter were then passed up to the " president " who would do his own thinning-out. I often wished that the critics of such competitions could have seen these men at work. The system was infallibly giving the competitor a fair deal.

Yet it failed for a period, nevertheless. The human factor took it by surprise.

This human factor was a man whom we must call by some name other than his own. Let it be Bispham. Bispham was the chief of the competition department—the " president." He sat at the desk at the head of the table. He apparently also sat elsewhere and did some powerful thinking, which opened up for him the prospect of easy money through the medium of the competitions. It was obvious that, if he himself sent in a number of entries, some of them were likely to come before him at his desk, particularly if he gave some indication to his staff as to the kind of entry likely to receive favourable consideration. For instance, he might have said that it was a long time since the winning line had had a political kick, he himself having sent in a number of entries with that same political kick. (I mention this not as a fact, but as an indication of how entries might be guided to his desk.)

The story is an example of how easy money in crime can beget laziness. Had he continued as he began, he might never have been found out.

He began by taking, for a companion and himself, a cheap little house in some crowded London area, and from there, under an assumed name, he sent in a batch of entries for the competition, for there was no limit to the number which one might send in, provided the necessary postal orders accompanied them. By slickness he contrived that one of his own entries came to his desk, and from there to the editor. It won him a three figure sum.

Now this process could not be repeated immediately from London, so Bispham and his companion took another weekly-tenancy house in a provincial town from which to send in another batch of efforts. Again he passed himself through as a winner, perhaps not of the first prize, but of one which made the trouble well worth while. So it went on, and might have continued if he had not jibbed at the trouble involved in securing his addresses. Why not, he asked himself, take an occasional rest by using an accommodation address ? There were plenty of little shops which, for a few shillings a week, would allow their premises to be used as an address.

So it happened—fairly successfully for a time. But he had not bargained for that person known as " the disappointed competitor," the man who wanted to see for himself that everything was all right. This man, who had no doubt heard the ever-persistent rumours that competition firms won their own prizes through a " stooge," called at an address from which Mr. Bispham had won a prize. Scarcely to his astonishment, he found the address to be an accommodation one.

By a few shrewd inquiries of the shopkeeper, he built up a picture of Mr. Bispham's appearance, and next day posted himself outside Pearson's offices. Again without surprise, he saw Bispham enter the building in the morning, go out at lunchtime and return in the early afternoon. Obviously an employee of the firm!

This was enough for the disappointed competitor. He went in and asked to see the managing director, whom he challenged on the matter. Of course, Pearson's knew nothing of what had been going on, and were soon able to convince their visitor that this was so. The result was that, later in the afternoon, Mr. Bispham was called down to an interview at which were two plain-clothes men from Scotland Yard.

The result was a prosecution, and Bispham went to prison ; but it left *Pearson's Weekly* in rather an awkward position. The story was bound to become a subject of talk with innuendoes that the competition was not all that it seemed. Accordingly, the firm decided to refer boldly to the case in their own paper, assuring readers, if assurance were needed, of their scrupulous regard for the honesty of the competition. The outcome, I believe, was much to the credit of the firm, which would not have been the case had they tried to hush it up. The " happy ship " had scored again.

It was whilst at Pearson's that I met John Hassall, the famous poster artist. We wanted a symposium for *Pearson's Magazine* on the influence of colour in our daily lives. My job was to see representative people on the subject, among them Lady Duff-Gordon (" Lucille," the fashion designer) and John Hassall. While talking to Hassall in his lofty studio, I asked him if there was any such thing as a humorous colour.

" Yes, spots are humorous," he said, " even black ones. That's why we laugh at a Dalmatian dog."

" Can you mention a tonic colour ? " I asked.

" Of course," he replied, " the colour of a good port is a tonic. That's why you hold it to the light before you drink it."

" But surely," I said, trying to catch him, " you do the same with a bottle of Bass ? "

" Ah," flashed Hassall, " but that's to see if there's any cork in it."

Most of us had some queer assignments at Pearson's, but I think the oddest of all fell to me. The chairman of the firm at that time was Sir George Riddell, later to become Lord Riddell, owner, more or less, of the *News of the World*. His breeziness at the board meetings was said to be a mild embarrassment to the other directors, for business was often held up until he had told them one or two of " his latest."

Sir George developed curiosity about a Sunday paper of that period, which, excellent as it may have been, was not too selective about the advertisements which appeared in it. It had an " Educational " column, and it was this which gave rise to curiosity on the part of Sir George. The column contained a number of advertisements of young French ladies offering to teach their fascinating language to the English ; there were ladies seeking companions with whom to practise fencing, and there were ladies anxious to do any kind of secretarial work to keep ravenous wolves from their doors.

So Sir George, for his personal satisfaction, asked P. W. Everett to put one of his men on to the job of personally investigating a few of these gems. The lot fell upon Mathias, meaning me. Mr. Everett displayed a little diffidence in handing the job to one so unsophisticated as myself, but I managed to put him at his ease.

I chose an address in Maiden Lane for my first investigation without seeing the humour of my choice. The lady had offered to teach French to English gentlemen, and it was with this well fixed in my mind that I knocked on the door of a flat high up in a none too salubrious building. A slight smell of cooking lurked about the passage, for it was lunch-time. I guessed it must be French cooking.

The door was opened by a charming young lady wearing a draughty-looking kimono of red silk, trimmed with black fur. I noticed no trace of a French accent as she asked me in and bade me be seated on one of those sink-in kind of settees. Sinking beside me, she soon cut short my inquiries about French lessons and said that what I really needed was a massage. A strategic withdrawal seemed imperative. At that moment, however, there came a spluttering, fizzing sound from the kitchen and she bounded out to rescue her lunch. This gave me my chance and I hurried out, calling that I would be around again in the evening.

This was but one of the advertisements I investigated, some presenting more difficult problems of extrication. In the end, I concluded that French ladies did not want to teach, nor fencing ladies to fence ; still less did starving secretaries want to work. And of such was my report to Sir George.

They were great days at Pearson's.

CHAPTER III

ANGLE ON AGENCIES

THERE are three kinds of Editorial agencies in Fleet Street—News, Photograph and Feature. To describe the functions of a great news agency such as Reuter's or the Press Association (now merged) would require a whole book. Its correspondents are in every corner of the world, and from them comes a never-ending stream of hot news which is relayed from London on subscription to newspapers everywhere.

The photographic agency supplies photographs to newspapers and periodicals at a fee graded according to the importance of the journal. This agency is also outside the scope of our book.

The feature agency is more our concern, for I have been intimately connected with it during much of my Fleet Street life. To some extent, the feature agency touches both news and photographs, in addition to its normal function of supplying features, so that the man on a feature agency has a good insight into newspaper matters generally. On the other hand, the newsman has but little acquaintance with the workings of feature agencies, which vary in size from the two-roomed office to the large organisations, the latter being countable on one hand.

A feature agency is what its name implies—an agency providing features, i.e., almost anything save news and advertisements.

In the days when papers ran to sixteen pages, and periodicals were as thick as dog-biscuits, editors thirsted for features of different kinds, from brief, catchy little things to the big features, such as life stories by people with lives worth writing about. Among these one might place famous detectives, crooks, stage people, cricketers, retiring magistrates, jockeys and politicians. As a rule, editors did not go into the highways and byways to seek guests for their columns, but relied mainly on feature agencies who hunted the social field with all the ardour of stoats.

The feature agency must not be confused with the " literary agency " or " authors' agency," although at points the two may overlap. The latter usually takes over the whole work of authors, chiefly fiction writers, charging a percentage on the prices obtained for their stories, long or short. In the case of a book, the agent guides it all the way from the typewriter to the tome. He sells the serial rights, i.e., its use in a newspaper or magazine before book publication ; he places the book with a publisher and fixes terms, and he arranges, if a book is filmable, for the film rights.

Many authors prefer to deal with their work themselves, submitting MSS. to editors and publishers according to their own judgment. A large proportion, however, choose to write their stories, send them off to their agent and hope for the best. The agent usually knows the market better than does the author, and is often aware of certain editors' immediate requirements. This the author would not know, and might well omit sending his MS. to the very editor who required it. Further, by using an agent, the beginner is saved the mortification of that periodical bump in his letter-box which means that one more editor has been consumed with regret.

Not all literary agents are boons, and an author should be wary in his choice of one. Some charge a preliminary fee before they begin to send the MS. on its rounds to editors, which means that the agent is all right, whether the story sells or not. This, in cases, may be justifiable, but the greatest danger for the author is the probability of selecting an agent who does not know his job and never will—the agent who does not study the editorial market but sends out stories regardless of suitability, thus being a nuisance to editors and an unsuspected handicap to his author.

How well I know it, because for a time I was selector of the famous *Evening Standard* series of short stories, with Leslie Marsh to give the final say. The series ran nightly for several years and kept up a uniformity of good fiction which was new to Fleet Street. Stories were submitted in large numbers, not only from agents but authors direct, and it amazed me to see how some of the literary agents, who should have known better, failed to study our requirements. Rarely did an *Evening Standard* story exceed 3,500 words, or fall below 2,000, yet stories regularly came in half as long again as any we had used, and many under our minimum.

Again, the *Evening Standard* never published stories of the handsome boy and girl type. The straight love story, indeed, was practically barred. But what did some of the agents do but slam in stories which could have sold nowhere except to popular women's journals! Of course, this lightened my work, for such stories were rejected at a glance. I have always imagined these delinquent agents to have a list of journals to which stories are submitted automatically. This I regard as grossly unfair to the authors who have entrusted their work to them.

Often reliable agents decline an author's work unless they see some promise of success. It is then up to the author not to seek a mediocre agent, but to handle his own stories and prove, as many have done, that the agent was wrong! Let it be borne in mind that no agent has a magic touch. If a story is good, an editor does not care a rap whether it comes from a literary agent or an unfrocked veterinary surgeon.

The feature agency does not, as a rule, handle matter on commission. It buys it outright from the authors, because it generally has a definite use for it through its syndicating department. I have described syndication in the previous chapter. In the present case, it means that the agency will buy a set number of serials and short stories yearly for the use of their established clients in various Provincial towns. This does not apply to more important features such as life stories, where a commission basis is usually arranged, taking into account the work which falls upon the agency. Not always is the subject capable of writing his own life story, for writing is a job of its own, with a long apprenticeship behind it. Therefore an agency often has to assign a man to " collaborate " with the subject, extracting the information as best he can.

As an instance I will quote the case of a detective's reminiscences which I once prepared. My difficulty was to keep him to the subject of the chapter on hand. We would be sitting together, perhaps at his house, or in a pub, while he talked and I made notes for subsequent writing up. This is the kind of thing which would happen :

Myself : I say, Parker, this is going to be a good story, and a murder at that. What happened after you followed your man into the main street ?

Detective : What about another drink ?

Myself : Good health. Now we had got to the main street—

Detective : That's right, and then the —— jumped on a tram.
Good health. Don't know what you think, but this beer seems
a bit flat to me.

Myself : I agree, we'll go somewhere else after this one. Meanwhile, we've got to where he jumped on a tram—

Detective : That's right, he did. But I happened to see a bicycle
standing outside a greengrocer's. It had a carrier in front,
with onions in it. Fond of 'em ?

Myself : Love 'em. And then—

Detective : Well, of course, I jumped on it without so much as a
by-your-leave to the greengrocer, and followed the tram. Speaking of bicycles, it was my young grandson's birthday yesterday.
He'd never had a bicycle, so the missus and I thought we'd get
him one. By heaven, he's coming around with his dad to-night.
We'll have to leave the rest until I see you again. Make it
Thursday.

This actually happened ; not once, but many times, and not
with one man, but many. Add to this our services in placing the
series of reminiscences with a newspaper, and a fifty-fifty basis
does not seem out of the way. Indeed, it was our general basis
for work of this kind.

As an illustration of the field covered by the feature agencies,
here is an example of a different kind. I was a partner of
Newspaper Features, Ltd., at the time when contact was
made with us by a breezy, genial fellow named Major Forbes-
Leith who proposed to drive a car from London to Quetta (India)
by road—with the exception of the Channel crossing and any other
short water journey which might be necessary. It looked a for-
midable undertaking, as indeed it was, for it entailed travelling
along unmade roads, or no roads at all, through wild and barbarous
country. Forbes-Leith asked us to undertake the newspaper
rights of the adventure, and to handle such messages and photographs as he was able to send through to us. He was taking two
companions to help with any difficulties and dangers that might
confront them.

We undertook to handle the expedition and set about interesting
newspapers in it. We decided to " syndicate " it. I mention
this because it is a good illustration of syndication. I went to
the *Evening Standard* first, and arranged with them to have ex-

clusive rights of publication in London and a hundred miles round
it.   Another member of the firm went up to Glasgow and fixed
up the feature with the *Record and Mail* people.   At Leeds the
paper was the *Yorkshire Evening News*.   So there we had three
non-conflicting newspapers for a start.

The expedition was to start from Piccadilly Circus, and after
a big luncheon at the Trocadero, attended by a well-known motor
magnate (whose make of car was being used) the trio drove out of
London with " London to Quetta " plastered over the car.   That
was the last we heard of Forbes-Leith for a long time.   Then
his messages and film-rolls began to arrive through devious
sources, and the feature was a great success, ending with a last
and glorious instalment about his arrival in Quetta.

Later, we handled in a similar way the Oxford University
Arctic Expedition so courageously led by a young man named
George Binney.   This bright and cherubic adventurer had passed
out of my mind until recently, when he became a front-page
story by being called to Buckingham Palace, to be privately
knighted by the King for a secret *coup* he brought off for the
Allies in Scandinavia.

Features can originate in strange ways.   A chance remark once
put me on to a most original one.   I was at the office of Hughes
Massie, prominent literary agent, one afternoon, talking over
some business matter with Miss Ruth Rogers, the clever " manager " of that then well-known firm.   Our business over, we found
ourselves chatting about the growing prevalence of titled people
breaking into print through the medium of professional " ghosts."
There were quite a number of these in Fleet Street at the time.
They would write a short article on some ordinary " silly season "
topic such as " Are Holidays Necessary ? " or perhaps something
more serious, then take it to some guinea-hungry titled person
to be signed.   Unfortunately, editors seemed quite ready to take
this kind of thing, and columns were graced daily by " distinguished authors " who had never written a line.

" Really, Mr. Shepherd," said Miss Rogers, " we shall have
Steve Donoghue writing a novel next! "

I made no reply but walked down the stairs in a dream.   Here
was an idea.   Steve was at the height of his fame at the time.   He
had won several Derbys and the phrase " Come on, Steve "

resounded in the land. Supposing Steve *did* write a racing story, and suppose it were serialised by a newspaper . . . ?

Now let me be quite clear about this. There was no question of getting the popular little jockey to pretend he had written a story ; I am sure Steve would have told me some home truths had I suggested it. What I had in mind was that Steve should provide the incident and background, and that the story should be written by a first-class author. I thereupon mentioned the matter to my old friend, the late E. C. Buley, who, as a sporting writer, was enjoying a reputation as " The New Nat Gould " (the late racing novelist). Buley liked the idea, and stroked his Mephistophelian beard with pleasure at the thought of collaborating with one who was his idol. I now had to see the idol.

I rang up a genial Irishman named McCarthy, who was " Robin Goodfellow," the *Daily Mail* racing correspondent, and asked if he could arrange for me to meet the celebrated jockey. As it happened, there was racing on the following Saturday at Alexandra Palace—" Ally Pally " to racing folk—and McCarthy promised to effect the introduction. The meeting took place in the weighing-in room—jockeys, saddles, bridles and the rest of it all around me. It was a new experience, and one from which I derived a considerable kick. The smallness of the jockeys made me feel a veritable Gulliver in Lilliput.

Steve agreed, partly out of good will, I'm sure, and at a later date everything was fixed up. Meanwhile I had seen Harry Ainsworth, editor of *The People*. He was enthusiastic about it, and the price—a high one—was decided upon.

In due course the serial appeared, with Buley's name subjoined. It was a good story and proved a great success. I often wonder if Miss Rogers ever read it!

The answer to the question—what is a Fleet Street character ? —could have been found in Ernest Buley. Like many industrious men, he always seemed to have plenty of time, which meant that we saw a great deal of him in Fleet Street, although he was actually working at home, turning out his incomparable racing stories. This period followed that during which he held various important editorial posts, including that of editor of the *Weekly* (now *Sunday*) *Dispatch*. He was a conspicuous figure, with his pointed beard and glittering eye. Extra distinction was added to him by his bowler hat, which, like so many journalists' *chapeaux*, had achieved it own shape, due in parts to use, the elements, and being sat upon.

This bowler hat played a minor part in an effort by Buley and myself to obtain an important feature which, however, did not mature. I myself had already made contact with the Retired Partner of an eminent bookmaking firm, which numbered most of the sporting aristocracy among its clients, whilst in Tattersall's Ring, Royalty had used its services. The reminiscences of its Retired Partner, therefore, promised to be a winner.

The R.P. lived in a select seaside resort, and it was here that I persuaded him to write, through me, a startling series of sporting memories. It was arranged that I should go down again a few days later to start on the *magnum opus*, which I did. The R.P., by the way, was a distinguished-looking man, more like a bishop than a bookie. He was a good talker and at once began to tell me good stories. At least, they would have been good if I could have understood them. As it was, they depended to a great extent upon a background of turf technique which was absolutely foreign to me. I know nothing about racing, a fact which soon became apparent to the R.P. At last the blankness of my face prompted him to say :

" Don't you think, Mr. Shepherd, that you ought to bring along someone who understands what I'm talking about ? "

His remark did not catch me by surprise ; I had anticipated him an hour before.

Well, of course, there was nothing for it but, once again, my old friend Ernest Buley ; and, once again, Buley jumped at it. I should say that there was no man in the country who knew so much of the intricacies of betting as did this shrewd old punter. Yes, Buley was the man. We arranged to go down and see the R.P. on the following Sunday.

Sartorial pride was not part of Buley's make-up. He dressed just as he pleased, so I had to give him a few delicate hints that we were going to see a distinguished old man in a not undistinguished new hotel. Buley ran his hand over his beard and said he quite understood. We were to meet at Croydon station on Sunday morning, as it suited us both, thence to proceed to the coast. In due course Buley turned up in a smart set of flannels and tweeds with a newness about them which suggested he had bought them for the purpose. But—and here was the horror of it—he was wearing his old bowler hat, which, unluckily, had now come asunder at the brim! Of course this presented a problem, as I pointed out. Buley laughed and said he'd be damned if he hadn't put it on absent-mindedly.

" Still, it will do all right," he said, giving it a brush with his coat-sleeve. " Good enough for a seaside place."

" Maybe," I said, " but not quite the thing for the red-carpeted show we're going to. How about leaving it somewhere and going without a hat ? "

" What, *me*—as bald as a coot—wandering about a windswept sea-front without a hat! " There was indignation in his voice. " Not —— likely ! "

Happily I saw a way out. " Here, try mine," I said, handing him my soft one. " I've plenty of hair, so it won't matter."

Fortunately it fitted him, so together we went to the left luggage office and deposited Hat No. 1 with a rather surprised clerk, to be collected later. With that we caught our train to the coast.

The Retired Partner was overjoyed when he found that he and Buley spoke the same language. He told us some good yarns, but all the best ones ended with an admonition that they should not go into the story. This was bad enough, but when he told us a few racy ones about Edward, Prince of Wales, laying bets with him at the rails, each one ending with " But of course that's not for print," we told each other with mutual glances that this interview with the Retired Partner would be our last.

That evening saw two deflated men at Croydon left luggage office, retrieving a murky bowler hat, making an exchange of headgear and passing out into a cruel street.

Fortunately " they " were open.

When Ernest Buley was editor of the *Weekly* (now *Sunday*) *Dispatch*, he was known in Fleet Street as an editor who didn't mind doing the difficult jobs himself. This was quite true, especially if there happened to be a spice of humour about them, as there was when he himself covered the visit of Hengler's Circus to Buckingham Palace. It was a Command Performance and the Press were to be excluded ; but Buley thought otherwise. He could, of course, have put a man on afterwards to interview the circus people, but, to use his own words, he " thought he could get a better angle on the story " by going there personally, ban or no ban.

I wonder how many editors there are to-day who would do as he did, and find a pub frequented by some of the circus band! This he did, and was soon on friendly terms with the drummer, the trombonist and the rest, including the band's boss. In the end he persuaded the latter to give him a place in the band for the afternoon, which would have been a better idea if Buley had been able to play a note on something or other. By this time, however, the boss was as enthusiastic as Buley, and solved the difficulty by suggesting that he should play the triangle. He couldn't go far wrong with an instrument which produced only one note, and that only now and then.

The band was to march before the circus procession up the Mall, playing for all they were worth, and there was Buley and his triangle as bold as the best of them. Thus he entered the Palace grounds and saw the whole show, sharing in the smiles which Very Important People cast upon them.

But the story never appeared. In those days Lord Northcliffe insisted on being informed, at his place at Sutton Court, of everything of importance which was going into the paper. Angrily he said that this story must be killed. The wishes of Royalty could not be flouted. So there it was ; and all Buley had out of it was a lesson on the triangle.

Crossword puzzles have become so familiar to us that it seems strange to recall the time when they were non-existent. As I happened to be instrumental in starting the rage in this country, I will give the story. I was with Newspaper Features at the time, when there entered a young American who had a feature to propose. It fell to me to see him, and I listened with interest to how the puzzle had " caught on " in America. But I was not impressed with the puzzle itself. It just appeared to me as some variation of the old acrostic. In fact, had it not been a craze in America, I doubt whether I should have considered the idea. However, I told our young friend to leave his specimens with me, promising to try solving one or two myself. It is worth bearing in mind that the day was Thursday.

A colleague and I were then living on the Kent Coast, doing

the double journey to Town and back each day. It gave us about a couple of hours each way in the train ; but never did that time pass so quickly as on that Thursday evening when we tried out the Crosswords. They were unquestionably " something different." The same thing happened on the Friday morning. We seemed to reach London in half the time.

That day I went round to the *Sunday Express*, then edited by Guy Pollock, with Arthur David as his right-hand man. I told them all about the puzzle, and my words to the American came back like an echo from the *Sunday Express* : " They are merely a new form of acrostic."

I told Pollock and David that I had thought the same twenty-four hours ago, but had become a convert overnight. In the end, they promised to do the same as I had done, and take the puzzles home to try them. On Saturday morning I had a ring from Arthur David asking me to go round and see him. I found him as enthusiastic as myself.

" They're absolutely fascinating," he said. " We'll buy half a dozen and start with one in to-morrow's paper."

HORIZONTALS

1. A coin (slang). 4. A tree. 7. Period. 8. Through. 9. Counters of votes. 11. Cosy little room. 12. Drainages. 16. Meaning three (prefix). 17. Snake-like fish. 18. An Oriental coin. 19. Parched.

VERTICALS

1. Wager. 2. Mineral substance. 3. Eminent political figure. 4. Inflicted retribution. 5. A title. 6. Possesses. 10. Grassland. 12. Home of a certain animal. 13. Before (poetic form). 14. Always (poetic form). 15. Cunning.

BRITAIN'S FIRST CROSSWORD

Introduced by the Author through the *Sunday Express*, November 2nd, 1924

" Splendid," I replied. " Which one are you using first ? "

He told me, adding : " By the way, it has the word *honor* in it, spelt in the American way. You might just take it back and Anglicise it. And hurry up with it."

I went blithely back to the office, little realising that such a job was easier said than done. I won't say any more than suggest you try yourself to put an extra letter into the middle of a Crossword.   Anyhow, I made a drastic reconstruction and it appeared in a new form in next day's *Sunday Express*.

Newspapers have a way of quickly discovering whether a feature is popular or not, and next week David said that their readers were " all over it."   Of course the *Express* had launched the feature with a fanfare, telling their readers how the craze was sweeping America.   This made other newspapers interested, and soon Crosswords crept into most of them.   We at Newspaper Features decided to syndicate them among Provincial papers, and soon we had thirty or forty newspapers printing them.   We sent them out in the form either of blocks or matrices, the latter being hard *papier maché* moulds from which the newspapers could take their own metal casts.

So there you have the beginning of the Crossword in this country.

My mention of matrices brings up an interesting point about syndication.   At one time, most small Provincial newspapers used to buy all their features in this form or in actual metal. Many still do so.   At the Northern Newspaper Syndicate, we had our own printing works where all matter was set up in type on the Linotype.   From this a matrix was made, and from the matrix, any number of columns cast, all standardised in size to fit the presses of the newspapers.   This saved much trouble for the latter, who simply put the columns straight into their formes.   These metal casts are called stereos.

The Northern Newspaper Syndicate sent a good deal of matter in stereo to overseas newspapers.   Thus it was all in the day's work to send a quarter of a ton of fiction, as in one instance, to the *Buluwayo Chronicle*.   In most cases, stereo metal was returnable, but overseas papers, such as the one mentioned, used the method as a means of buying metal for their own purposes.

CHAPTER IV

FLEET STREET CHAPS

WHO, you ask, are Fleet Street Chaps? For our purpose they are the work-a-day men who form the background of a work-a-day street. They are reporters, sub-editors, free-lances, feature writers, artists, editors. They are men who know how to work and how to play.

The playing-fields of Fleet Street are mainly its taverns, and many a wordy game is played in them. Dr. Johnson, Oliver Goldsmith, Dickens, Thackeray played much the same games in Fleet Street as are played to-day. There was Dr. Johnson at the " Cheshire Cheese," Thackeray at the " Cogers," Dickens and Tennyson at the " Cock Tavern." Tennyson especially loved his " Cock Tavern," as this passage from his " Will Waterproof " shows :

> " Oh, plump head waiter of the *Cock*,
> To which I most resort,
> How goes the time ? 'Tis five o'clock ?
> Go fetch a pint of port!
> And let it not be such as that
> You set before chance comers,
> But one whose father grape grew fat
> On Lusitanian summers."

I am not one who believes that the standard of wit of these " giants " excelled that which maintains in Fleet Street to-day. Indeed, judged by much that has been preserved, it was a good deal inferior. Many of the epigrams thrown off were puerile, whilst the " cod " epitaphs so fashionable at one period were bad enough to make their subjects turn in their graves before they arrived there.

The subject of turning in graves impels me to quote Anthony Praga's crack about war-time meals. " They are enough," he said, " to make Mrs. Beeton turn in her grave-y."

Praga is the son of Alfred Praga, at one time President of the Miniaturists' Society. His mother was Mrs. Alfred Praga, the well-known Edwardian writer. He is a Jew of distant Polish origin, and enjoys Jew jokes as well as anybody.

Tony once shone in the *Sunday Express*, where he was writing a brilliant series of two-column cameos under the title of " Love Stories of the Great." These were followed by another series which consisted of famous novels boiled down to the length of a short story. For making the unread well-read they were as functional as Lamb's " Tales from Shakespeare." But they drew from Gwyn Evans, one of the writers of " Sexton Blake " stories, a slightly wicked Clerihew which delighted Fleet Street. (Before giving it I should mention that a " stick " is the printers' term for a few inches of type.) Here it is :

> " Anthony Praga
> Would condense the Forsyte Saga
> To a couple of ' sticks '
> For ten-and-six."

Gwyn Evans was well-known in Fleet Street, where he was a law to himself. Tall and dreamy, wispy, ethereal, Gwyn died quite young, leaving a world in which he always seemed something of a stranger. It was odd that such a gentle, poetical man should have been an author of the " Sexton Blake " thrillers, beloved by readers from schooldays to senility, but he turned them out with incredible facility, not only with inspiration, but with his abnormal speed on the typewriter.

Kindly as he was, he could at times write with acid instead of ink. He was an ardent Rationalist ; he believed in nothing that was not proved, and his tilts at organised religion were often confounding. Perhaps his best tilt of all was against a distinguished cleric who was not only a pillar of the Church, but a column each week in a newspaper, for which he received a cheque which would have blinded most newspapermen. Gwyn could not resist writing these unkind and most untrue lines :

> " Said the Very Reverend Dean Inge,
> ' To my faith I cling ' ;
> Then turned with a wink
> To the Street of Ink."

He told me that he sent a copy to his victim, which I doubt. In any case I'm sure that master of acerbity would merely have been amused.

Gwyn, unworldly as he was, could always deal with any of the financial emergencies with which Fleet Street often confronts those who work in it. Thus he told me of how he once found himself " a little near the knuckle " on a Thursday. He was doing " Sexton Blakes " at the time and was due to deliver a story which he had not even begun ; and the money was essential to his immediate programme.

He rose early on the Friday morning, and wrote the first and last chapters of the story ; then, taking the middle part of an old typescript, he made a sandwich which had all the appearance of a fully completed story. This he took to his editor, who, he knew, had a way of glancing at the beginning and end of a story and leaving further reading until later. The editor glanced at it and gave Gwyn the expected chit wherewith to collect his money from the cashier.

By Monday morning, Gwyn had completed the middle part. Bursting into his editor's room, he exclaimed :

" I'm awfully sorry, but I got my copy mixed up on Friday, and must have given you some old stuff. Here is what I meant to bring."

All was well.

The best story of Gwyn's financial acumen, however, concerns the exploit of the Albert Memorial and the Hard-boiled Egg. It may seem trivial, but it is illustrative of the odd, boyish mind which belongs to so many Fleet Street men. Gwyn, who never needed money, but always wanted it ; who earned plenty and spent about the same, was face to face with one of the usual financial crises. It was essential that he should have a few guineas next morning. Ordinary ways of getting the money did not appeal to him, and, as you could then buy hard-boiled eggs in buffets, Gwyn bought one that evening. Then, accompanied by a lady friend, he went to the Albert Memorial and sat down on the plinth steps, complete with his hard-boiled egg.

Next, he began to toss the egg from one hand to another, keeping all the time a Gandhi-like composure. Meanwhile the lady went to the nearest policeman, who happened to be just outside the gates of Kensington Gardens.

" Oh, Officer," she said, " there's a man behaving in an extraordinary manner on the steps of the Memorial."

" Nothing really wrong, I suppose ? " queried the policeman, saying that in any case he would go and see what it was all about. There he saw Gwyn, still tossing his egg to and fro. The officer could not call to mind any law forbidding a man to do what he liked with a hard-boiled egg, even on the steps of the Albert Memorial, but, as a small crowd had gathered, he had to say something. He asked Gwyn what it was all about.

" Well, I happen to belong to the Society for the Veneration of Ancient Monuments," explained Gwyn, " and each year one of us does this—at a different monument, of course. It was Cleopatra's Needle last year. Sort of rite, you know."

The policeman could do nothing except tell Gwyn that he had been at it long enough to serve the intentions of any society born of man, and walked away. Whereupon Gwyn strode off with his egg ; but only to the nearest telephone kiosk, from where he rang up the *Daily* ——. (No, I daren't mention it.)

" Gwyn Evans here. Good story. Chap on Albert Memorial tossing a hard-boiled egg about. Some peculiar rite, or something. What ? No, I can't do the story myself. Busy on something else, but you can send a man along. If the egg bloke has gone, your man can ask the nearest policeman who was questioning him when I came to 'phone you."

This is a normal procedure when a newspaperman otherwise engaged stumbles across a story, so along went the man from the paper. He had, of course, to fall back on the constable for the story, which was confirmed. Furthermore, it was printed, and next morning Gwyn went round and received three guineas from a grateful newspaper.

After all, as Gwyn said to me when I discussed the ethics of the affair with him, there actually *had* been a chap behaving extraordinarily at the Memorial!

Reverting to Tony Praga, there should be on record his classic crack about James Wentworth Day. As everyone knows, or should do, J. Wentworth Day was one of our foremost writers on country topics—farms, countryfolk, natural history, hunting.

One day, in the " Cheshire Cheese," he had been giving one of his not unusual dissertations on the chase, when Tony, who doesn't know a horse from a hen-coop, said : " Jimmy, old boy, I'm afraid you suffer from Tally-Hosis."

There was, until he died a few years ago, a much-liked man in Fleet Street named Herbert Bailey. He was editor of the British United Press, a news agency better known as the B.U.P. He was probably the most voluble man Fleet Street has ever known. Herbert had talked to us one night in the " Falstaff " for " a full hour by Shrewsbury clock," as the original Falstaff might have said, when Praga, itching to put in a word of his own, said : " Herbert, you are just an impediment in everybody else's speech."

I imagine that this remark would have been a classic had it been made by Dr. Johnson two centuries ago and come to us as :

" Sir," said Dr. Johnson, " you are nothing but an impediment in other people's speech."

In listening to the genial, stocky, imperturbable Eric Sisley, the stranger might well need an interpreter, for he has a way of referring to things by strange names. Thus, if he speaks of a B.B.C. man being good at the " groan-box," the initiated know he means the microphone. Liquid refreshment in general is " pongelo " ; an individual drink a " snort " ; and a pub a " snort-shop." Equally amusing is his way of using only the first letter of the first part of a word, leaving you to understand what he means. If you know him it is not difficult. Speaking of a bore, for instance, he will say he is a " p-lential nuisance," which means, of course, " pestilential."

With intimates he goes further. Speaking to me one day of a brush he was having with the requisitioning authorities about his country cottage, he said he felt secure because " P is N P of the L." He did not need to tell me that he meant " possession is nine points of the law."

The sartorial standards of the Street are low, for newspapermen have little regard for clothes and far less for hats, which have a positive genius for losing their shape when on a journalistic head. An exception to this was J. Wentworth Day, easily the best-dressed man of his era. Clothes seemed part of Jimmy Wentworth Day's life. Being concerned mainly in writing about rural matters, he spent a good deal of his time in the country and looks it. His complexion was the obvious result of Fenland winds, while his moustache was like a well-trimmed hedge. Usually he appeared in the dress of a country gentleman come to town— immaculately creased tweeds and a bowler hat clearly built by Lock. Periodically he looked the sporting squire, as he did one day after his return from a thousand-mile horseback tour of farms, about which he wrote for the *Daily Telegraph*, and which he described in his recent book, "Farming Adventure." On this occasion he arrived amongst us in a bright tweed riding jacket and breeches, a canary waistcoat and a stock in which nestled a gold tie-pin representing a game-cock, with ruby eyes.

I was talking with Peter Burnup, of the *News of the World*, in the old " Cheshire Cheese " when Jimmy entered. Burnup gave him a quick glance of recognition and said :

" Hello, Jimmy. Going to a funeral, I see."

Day was as amused as anyone, for he relished this kind of thing. Those of us in Fleet Street who can turn a verse frequently produce good-natured lampoons about each other. Here is one I wrote about Jimmy Day, who was a great friend of mine :

DEBONAIR DAY

" You were mentioning ' Debonair Day,' sir ?
   I happen to be that man.
If it's information you want, sir,
   I'll give you the best that I can.

The reason they call me that way, sir,
   Is mainly because of my togs,
With a sporting turn in buttons,
   And ties with their patterns of dogs.

I rarely am seen in a great-coat,
   Of worsted or tweed or of fleece,
For I'm not so much dressed by the garment,
   The thing that makes *me* is my crease.

And when the Last Chapter is written,
   When Life's thrilling canter is run,
And I am at last in some Place where
   A dog-whip's as good as a gun—

Be it Heaven or somewhere quite different,
    Or be it wherever it may,
There's one thing I'll always maintain, sir—
    I'll be Debonair J. Wentworth Day.

NOTE (POST MORTEM)

But they finished his ' Debonair Day ' stuff,
    For reasons he's still trying to probe,
When they bowled him a really swift one
    By fitting him up in a robe.

And they don't go a-fishing where he's gone,
    Nor can you shoot stars with a gun,
And you can't put a crease in a robe, so
    Debonair Jimmy is done."

CHAPTER V

MORE FLEET STREET CHAPS

NUMEROUS are the invitations to important functions received in newspaper offices. In normal times, many a reporter becomes bored with attending luncheons and dinners with speeches, and shudders when people say how lucky he is. Think of the food ; think of the wine, they say! He thinks of them and shudders again. I have even known men so tired of it that they have tried to dodge the Lord Mayor's banquet.

The most enjoyable affair it was ever newspapermen's luck to attend was the drawing of the Irish Sweepstake in Dublin. I was never there, but knew many who were. It lasted most of a week, and the hospitality was simply transcendental. There was a host of newspapermen there, and not one was allowed to spend any money—not if the Sweep authorities could help it. They were put up in the chief hotels, the food was Ireland's best, which is saying something, and the wines as choice as they were plentiful. A journalist sitting in his hotel lounge had merely to look as though he would like a Corona Corona for a waiter to swoop down with a box of them. Champagne flowed as consistently as the Liffey, morning, noon and night.

One day a number of happy journalists decided to sneak off to the races at the Curragh, instead of conforming to the pre-arranged entertainments. Somehow the Sweep authorities heard of it, and when the time came for them to go, they were escorted to a small fleet of Rolls-Royces waiting especially to take them to the Curragh!

We in Fleet Street hailed the Sweepstake heroes on their return, and listened avidly to their stories of Irish hospitality. We regarded them in the nature of survivors, feeling sure they must have left many dead upon the field.

Of course the Sweepstake people knew what they were doing. Those were the days before our Government aunties forbade any mention of the Irish Sweep in the Press, days when almost every

Englishman was thrilled to the marrow by what he read about the Sweep, in which, as likely as not, he held a ticket. The British Press was the Sweep's best advertisement.

In the matter of wines at functions, I think Jimmy Dunn and I " scooped the kitty " when we went to a luncheon given by the International Wine-tasters' Conference at the Savoy. James Dunn, it should be mentioned, was " R. E. Corder," of the *Daily Mail,* writer of a brilliant daily feature called " The Seamy Side " which was a series of human write-ups of the proceedings at Magistrates' Courts. Dunn was the pioneer of this kind of feature, which is still popular in several London newspapers. Jimmy was a Public Relations Officer at the War Office. Before going there, he was, in Fleet Street, the complete example of what is called " a familiar figure."

He was welcome in every company, partly because of his ruddy countenance which exuded cheerfulness, and partly for the epigrams which positively trickled off his tongue. " Fleet Street is a land flowing with ink and money " was one of them. Another : " Some men, cricketers and navvies, look well in belts. American business men don't."

This epigrammatic twist has been inherited by his son, Denis Dunn, successful writer of humorous features. It was Denis who said, when seeing a number of callow journalists in a Fleet Street milk bar : " It used to be ' one over the eight ' ; now it's ' one under the udder '."

*   *   *

The International Wine-tasters' Conference was a moveable occasion held annually in different European capitals by turn. It was attended by many famous gastronomes such as André Simon, " The Prince of French Wine-tasters." At these conferences were tasted—and spat out into silver cuspidors—all the finest vintages coming into circulation. Prices were fixed for the millionaires who would eventually drink them. Their labours over, the Wine-tasters gave a luncheon to the Press.

I went on the *Sunday Dispatch* invitation card ; Jimmy Dunn for the *Daily Mail.* When you think that the best brains and palates in Europe had been at work for days, selecting the wines, you can imagine that this was no ordinary lunch. In another way, too, it was extraordinary, but we were not to know that until we had eaten it.

Before each of us, on the table, was a mysterious envelope, not to be opened until the lunch was over, when it proved to contain the reasons for certain wines being provided with certain dishes. Or, rather, it was the other way about, for we were told that the *dishes* had been chosen to go with the *wines*, and not *vice versa* as is usually the case. The fish had been described in the menu as " Crimped Salmon." This, we learned, was chosen and specially prepared to go with a certain wine. The salmon had been caught that morning at Christchurch, incised with a silver knife, placed in a tank of sea-water, and hurried to London as the only conceivable adjunct to the amber delight which we drank with it.

Another item described in the book of words was " A dish of West Country veal, cooked over an oak fire and served with young broad beans in cream." And that, my masters, was the only thing calculated worthy of the particular *Vin de Bourgogne* with which it was served.

I feel sure that if Bill Taylor, editor of the *Sunday Dispatch* at the time, had known what lay behind that invitation card, he would have gone himself. Certainly the *Sunday Express* did not hand the ticket to a second-rater. No. The genial Lord Castlerosse represented them, and Dunn and I watched, as it were, the " roseate hues of early dawn " steal into his broad face as the lunch progressed.

When the last heavenly brandy had been dispatched, Jimmy and I walked out into the Strand. We had no wish to part; the question was, where should we go? We thought of a well-known wine-house across the way, but our ideas of wine had become exalted during the past hour and we ruled it out. Finally we did the only thing possible to return to normal. We took a taxi to the " Cheshire Cheese " and ordered two tankards of beer. It seemed the only way.

Jimmy Dunn was responsible for one of the best Fleet Street stories ever told. There had been a train smash in the Midlands and Dunn was sent to cover it, accompanied by Harold Pemberton, son of Sir Max Pemberton, a lovable fellow who lost his life later when the *Daily Express* plane crashed into a Scottish mountain side. Reaching the scene of the train smash, they found there was nothing in it. A goods train had been derailed, with none of those fatalities which, alas, make a good story. They discovered, however, that three of the waggons were conveying part of a menagerie, and that a number of animals had escaped. Here was a story handed to them on a silver plate, and Jimmy rang the *Daily Mail*. There was not much time to lose before the first edition went to press, so Jimmy wasted none of it on what should have been the preliminaries to his story.

" There's nothing in the smash," he said hurriedly, " but listen. Snakes and alligators are roaming the countryside . . ."

The night news-editor was an understanding chap.

" That's all right, Jimmy," he said. " Take my tip and go to bed. Best thing, you know . . ."

Dunn, exasperated, began again.

" Snakes and alligators—"

Again the night news-editor cut it short. " Do please go to bed," he said tersely.

Then Harold Pemberton had a go at it : " Snakes and alligators—"

" What! You as well! For heaven's sake, both of you go to bed," he shouted.

Eventually Jimmy told him what he had not mentioned in his haste, that a menagerie had been derailed. Only then did the night news-editor see that the story was quite non-alcoholic. It was on the front page of the *Daily Mail* the next day, and Fish, the news editor of the paper, gave Dunn and Pemberton a bonus of £5 each for getting so good a story.

Another unusual Press function I attended, was a caviare party given by the London importers of this gift of the gods to mark the opening of the new season. The invitation cards were things of beauty, with the Russian Royal Emblem done in gold. The card also intimated that we should have the honour of meeting the Grand Duke. This promised to be thrilling, and so it was, even though the Grand Duke happened to be a huge stuffed sturgeon. Being a lover of caviare, I appreciated the sight of long tables on which were dotted little dishes of this luxury which you could pick up at will. There was black caviare, red caviare and a caviare called *Perles du Volga*, rightly named, for the " units " were nearly as large as pearls. The only drinks were Vodka and Schnapps, which caught a few of us by surprise. I found myself in the company of Eric Maschwitz and Walford Hyden, of Café Colette fame, and a good time was had by all. Functions such as these leave the Lord Mayor's Banquets cold.

Well to be remembered was an evening given by the Anglo-Danish Society at Grosvenor House. In this case it was a *smörrebrod* supper, which meant a slap-up feast of Danish hors d'œuvres, flown that day from Copenhagen. The drink was Tuborg lager served from a chromium wagon which produced it ice-cold. We were asked to accept the elegant glasses we had used, and passers-by must have been mystified to see us walking down Park Lane, hugging our glasses.

Another unusual Press invitation was to a luncheon aboard a new ship, well out to sea in the English Channel. I went on behalf of the Central News, the occasion being a maiden trip by a new Southern Railway boat which was to ply on the Channel Islands route. We joined the ship at Southampton in the morning and set off, with the Mayor of Southampton and the ship's builders aboard, into the sunlit Channel, to ease up, or whatever sailors call it, while a luncheon and speeches occurred. There was a new and painty smell about the ship which did not appeal to the poorer sailors among us, but there was a free bar which to some extent neutralised this.

I wrote a column in the train on the return journey and handed it to the Central News, who wired it to Guernsey, where it appeared in the *Guernsey Star* the next day. The story at least goes to show what the Central News would do to please an individual client.

Perhaps the most charming man who ever walked Fleet Street was the lean and scholarly-looking Henry Doig, who died a few years ago. The news that yet another newspaperman has gone off on his Last Assignment is not unusual in Fleet Street, which cuts off many men before their time. I hardly dare count the men I have known intimately who have left us while still in their forties. Irregular hours, chance meals, hard work and hard play are no friends of longevity. To last out in Fleet Street you must come from where they breed men, not mice.

But the news of Henry Doig's death affected Fleet Street in an unusually profound way. Generally such news makes but a short impression ; with Doig it was different. It really seemed as though his spirit haunted the place, for his name was on men's lips for many a day. Even to-day he is often discussed, not that there was anything spectacular in his life, but because of his wit, his literary craftsmanship and the readiness with which he gave advice to many, from young subs to elderly editors. He did not suffer fools gladly, but even these loved him. He and I were especial friends, and when he died I wrote the following sonnet, which appeared in the *Newspaper World* :

> " Let other pens in Fleet Street pause awhile
> In mem'ry of a pen which now is still,
> Of faultless epigram and envied skill
> Which taught the very stylist what is style.
> In mem'ry of a voice, and that lost smile,
> Which, in its showing, surely did distil
> The essence of the mind which urged the quill,
> Now quiet, no more the reader to beguile.
>
> Henry is dead. Yet, through the length of days
> To come, his spirit shall be surely ours
> Who met him in the places where scribes meet.
> So let it be. And that well-balanced phrase
> And gleaming wit, dispensed in quiet hours
> To friends, shall be fond echoes in the Street."

Doig was equally at home with short stories, articles or news. He was also a barrister, although he rarely mentioned it. He felt it put him rather higher than the ordinary working journalist, which he was content to be. It was because of his legal knowledge that Bernard Falk, then editor of the *Sunday Dispatch*, gave him the job of overlooking the paper legally on Saturday mornings. Libels can easily creep into a paper, which is why every newspaper has its own barrister whose responsibility it is to see that the pages are libel-proof. This, as you can imagine, is no light job on a newspaper running at pre-war size.

Doig was able to tell many stories of Bernard Falk, among them the following. The time was just subsequent to the release of Horatio Bottomley from prison, where he had served a seven years' sentence for the Victory Bonds fraud, whilst he was editor of *John Bull*. The *Sunday Dispatch* bought his life story for a high figure—I believe it was £20,000—and ran it over many weeks under the title " I Have Paid, But——."

One morning, as Henry was going through that week's instalment, something told him he had read it before, that it was old stuff. By luck he was able to find a copy of a little book Bottomley had written many years before, and there was the identical part of his life story, almost word for word. Henry took the book, with the galley proofs of the instalment, and put them before Falk.

Falk scrutinised them, then looked up at Doig.

" D'you know, Henry," he said slowly, in his deliberate Lancashire voice, " I'm *beginning* to think this chap Bottomley's a rogue ! "

Whatever Bottomley may have been, he was a great journalist. He conducted *John Bull* with such virility and acumen that made the practised periodical proprietors sit up and blink, for, almost overnight, he achieved a circulation such as they themselves had merely dreamed about.

No market has a greater variety of traders than you find in Fleet Street, and by " traders " is here meant traders of the written word. Putting aside newspapermen on well-known journals, you may meet men on all kinds of specialist publications known mainly to those whose interests they serve. That man having a snack at the " Falstaff " bar writes for the *Farmer and Stockbreeder*. The man next to him is on the *Fur Trades Gazette*. Another strolls in. He is Mac, of the *Morning Advertiser*, the daily newspaper of the licensing trade, a genial fellow as befits his calling. The paper is not on sale in the ordinary way, but is to be found in hotels and pubs all over the country.

If you want to buy or sell a pub, engage a barmaid or a chef, " live in or sleep out," your medium is the *Morning Advertiser*. If you are a backer of horses, the *Morning Advertiser* will not lead you far astray with its tips ; and you will find in it much news of the actual City of London which you do not read elsewhere. It is the second oldest paper in London. *The Times* is the oldest.

Or perhaps you may meet rugged-faced Tim Sedgwick, of a sporting paper—Tim of the inevitable brown tweeds with a catapult in one of his pockets. He is an inveterate practical joker ; not that his catapult is a joke, as many a London pigeon in a quiet square has discovered too late. Tim's best joke was brought off in the almost sacred precincts of the Temple, that ancient, much-blitzed lawyers' area behind the western end of Fleet Street.

Here Tim was walking with a friend one day when he saw two of His Majesty's judges emerging from some chambers and turning into Middle Temple Lane, on their way to the Law Courts on the other side of Fleet Street. Now Tim, who is a countryman, can probably get nearer to a bird or beast than can most men. In any case, one can almost stumble over the fat, aldermanic pigeons in the Temple. There was a group of them pecking chaff in the Lane, and in a split second Tim dropped his hat over one of them, and withdrew into a small court from where he could watch events.

With heads bent in conclave, the judges—one of them the late Lord Justice Scrutton—came up the Lane, then suddenly stopped in their tracks. A hat was dancing about in front of them. Really ! Most disconcerting ! So early in the day, too ! Each edged the other back a little when their embarrassment was relieved by the pigeon, who managed to flap out from under the hat. Whereupon the judges proceeded in their previous solemnity to administer His Majesty's law, supremely regardless of Tim's now static tile. No doubt they had a dry crack about it over the dry sherry at lunch-time.

The Law and Journalism are closely intermingled, not only socially at the Law Courts end of the Street, but in the sense that every trial of importance is covered by the Press. There are many journalists who have spent much of their working life in reporting trials, while quite a few claim to have sat through most of the great murder trials of the past twenty years. They will tell you first-hand stories, which have never seen the light of print, of such famous figures as Justices Avory, Darling, Charles or Birkett, or of Marshall-Hall, Sir Patrick Hastings and other great lawyers.

The only murder trial I attended was that of Mrs. Barney, who was charged at the Old Bailey with shooting a man at a mews flat in the West End. The trial ended in an acquittal, the shooting being proved an accident. I sat in the Press box among a number of newspapermen, including the late James Douglas and Hannen Swaffer. Over my shoulder one morning I saw George Arliss sitting in the public seats behind me, looking as though he had just stepped out of one of his own films. At the resumption of the trial after lunch, someone evidently purloined his seat, and I found him sitting next to me in the Press box. Some kindly disposed newspaperman had come to his aid. We had a few whispered words, but talking is fiercely frowned upon at murder trials.

At the Court of Criminal Appeal, in the Law Courts, I heard the appeals of murderers whose names will live long in the annals of crime. They were Patrick Mahon, Pierre Vaquier and the ill-fated couple in the " Cleft Chin " crime. I have heard newspapermen say that they have often been more impressed by an Appeal than by the case itself. The Appeal Court represents the Ultimate in Law. The man you see before those three robed judges is probably taking his last look at the outside world. If his appeal is dismissed, as most of them are, nothing can save him but the Home Secretary's reprieve, the prospects of which are infinitesimal.

Patrick Mahon had been found guilty of murdering Emily Kaye in a bungalow on the Crumbles coast. It was a particularly gruesome murder, for he had cut up the body and disposed of much of it in various ways. He might have been entirely successful, had not his suitcase, containing blood-stained clothing, been found in a railway left-luggage office. Remarkably handsome as he was, he appeared an insignificant figure as he stood between two immensely tall warders in the dock and heard Lord Hewart's concluding words :

" . . . Therefore the Appeal is dismissed."

As in a dream he walked from the dock. His days were numbered.

Pierre Vaquier, a Frenchman who knew little or no English, had been sentenced to death for poisoning the licensee of the " Blue Anchor " at Byfleet, because he considered him as " the husband in the way." Dapper to the point of effeminacy, with a well-oiled, pointed beard, he seemed to follow closely a series of legal arguments which he could not possibly have understood. When, at the end, he sensed that it was all over, and felt the warder's hand upon his shoulder, he shot an accusing finger at his judges and hurled at them a torrent of imprecation in French. A moment later he, too, had gone.

It was Marshall-Hall who secured the acquittal of the solicitor Greenwood, who was tried at Hereford Assizes for the murder of his wife. The great advocate's eloquence and the weight of evidence combined to make Greenwood a free man. It was not long afterwards that another solicitor, living in a small township not far away, was also charged with the murder of his wife by poisoning. His name was Major Armstrong, and he was found guilty at the same Assize Court.

At that time there was a prevalent rush to obtain sensational crime stories, and a feature agency I knew conceived what might be called a big idea. It was that the solicitor Greenwood (who died not long afterwards) should be present at the trial of Armstrong and write his impressions. It was a ghoulish idea, but well in keeping with the demands of certain newspapers in those days, when responsible editors would go to an Assize city where a murder trial was in progress, and hold an auction to decide which of them should have the life story of the prisoner, if he or she were acquitted. The highest bidder had it, and the representative of the acquitted person was there to see that all was properly fixed financially. Things like these are of the past, but not a long-distant past.

It was not unnatural, therefore, that Greenwood should be persuaded to go to Hereford to witness a trial so akin to his own. A Sunday newspaper had promised a fat sum for the story, and Greenwood and an agency man duly arrived in Hereford. By the influence which a pressman can often exert, they reached the door of the court in which Armstrong was fighting for his life before the penetrating eyes of Mr. Justice Darling. An usher opened it, disclosing, with the suddenness of a theatre curtain, the grim drama which was being played.

For Greenwood this was enough. He gave one look at the scene, so similar to that in which he had lately been the central figure. Then he backed away and flatly refused to enter. This attitude he maintained, and so the " big idea " became a fiasco.

It is difficult to say just how this sensation-mongering declined ; but it certainly did. It may have been that newspapers, with one accord, tired of the big prices which were being paid to the representatives of people who had figured in sensational cases. Whatever the reason, there was a sudden disinclination to publish stories by murder acquittees, and young girls who had figured in prosecutions against public men.

*   *   *

Stories and repartee among newspapermen belong to a *genre* of their own. The so-called suggestive story is almost unheard in the Street, not because of prudishness, believe me, but because ·most of them are unutterably dull and all newspapermen are hard-boiled. They can usually tell what is coming before the narrator is half-way through his tale, and they just don't want to be bothered with it. The Stock Exchange is supposed to be the cradle of the doubtful story, and there is some truth in this. On more than one occasion when a City man has been among us, he has inevitably thought we would be pleased by a string of murky stories.

There are enough amusing stories belonging to the Street so that there is no call for invented ones. Even when an apocryphal yarn is heard, it usually has a dash of fact about it. Stories of reporters and editors, cub and sub- respectively, go the rounds regularly. There is one about the raw sub-editor of a Yorkshire paper who had to put a heading to a particularly meaty news-story. A man in Leeds had run amok and killed his wife ; then, dashing out of the house with a hatchet, had brained the first policeman he met. After that he had flung himself to death under an oncoming lorry. In a burst of understatement, the sub called the story : " LEEDS MAN'S STRANGE CONDUCT."

Then there was the small-town reporter who always began his report of the local football match with : " At the football match last Saturday . . ." Eventually, the editor pleaded with him. Would he, for the love of heaven, start in a different way ? It happened that next week he had to do a hard-luck story of how the local team lost by a fluke goal. Bearing in mind his editor's injunction, he began : " Cheese was never harder than when the Dribblers lost by the odd goal at the football match last Saturday."

There is also the story of the cub reporter who was a devil of a lad for his facts. He was sent to do a human story of the scene outside a gaol while an execution was taking place within. This is how he began :

" The sun was shining and birds twittered in the trees outside Blankton's grisly gaol as John Smith, plasterer, aged 55, walked from the condemned cell to pay the extreme penalty, *viz.*, Death."

Such stories of local papers always go down well, and there are many in circulation in Fleet Street, especially as some of these journals take themselves so seriously. Thus it is attributed to the *Skibbereen Eagle* that it once began its leader with : " We have repeatedly warned Russia . . ." while another remote paper said patronisingly : " Far be it from us to embarrass the Government . . ."

Stories of this kind are the breath of life to Fleet Street, though perhaps lacking point to the " civilians," as Jimmy Dunn once described a bunch of strangers in the " Cheshire Cheese " to Hayter Preston and myself.

Hayter Preston is responsible for much that is good in *Cavalcade*, and is one of the finest prose writers in present-day Fleet Street. If you meet Preston, you are sure of something to remember afterwards. Thus, a small group was once discussing some ethical subject which brought up a reference to original sin.

" Yes, but what *is* sin ? " asked somebody. " How would you define it ? "

Preston was with us, and a definition was at once forthcoming.

" Sin, my boy," he said, " is an ecclesiastical term for pleasure."

CHAPTER VI

ARTISTS AND OTHERS

THE artists' place in Fleet Street is important, and their functions many. Between them, they cover everything in newspapers and periodicals save photographs and the printed word. There are cartoonists who make us laugh, and cartographers who make us look at war-maps, artists who illustrate stories, commercial artists who illustrate advertisements, and joke artists who illustrate the funny side of life. Some are in jobs ; others are free-lances, making more money by working at their own desks than at someone else's.

I have collaborated with many artists in Fleet Street, and if anyone tells me they are an irresponsible lot, I am only being told what I know. They find life an amusement, even though it is going badly with them at the moment—attributable, perhaps to the joy they derive from their work. They have no need for scheduled relaxation, for their work is relaxation in itself. When the bank doors shut behind the bank clerk he does not spend his off-time doing columns of figures ; nor does the accountant account. But the artist and his pencil are always companions.

Take Will Farrow, for instance, that care-free sprig of Australia, who came over here as a soldier in the last war and forgot to return. He has only to see an amusing or interesting face and he is surreptitiously sketching it, usually on the inside of a cigarette carton for want of more suitable material. He will buy quite a number of packets during an evening just to draw caricatures on them. They have almost become his favourite medium! Sidney Potts and Jack McCail, who has done the cover of this book, are two others who laugh with their pencils when the day's work is done.

Among the artists with whom I have collaborated is Tom Cottrell, who is what one would call an all-round man. He has done Parliamentary cartoons and once deputised for Strube on the *Daily Express*, but his real metier is doing illustrated jokes for a variety of publications. My relations with Cottrell, apart from friendship, have been largely those of an unofficial agent, placing his work and occasionally supplying a bright idea for features.

I once arranged a Cottrell feature with the *Daily Express*, called "London Guy'd." It consisted of streets and parts of London represented daily by funny and sometimes cryptic drawings. Thus, a famous thoroughfare was represented by a fierce wife plucking a long hair from her hen-pecked husband's coat. (Got it?) Another sketch showed a monocled dude, in prison garb, sitting glumly in a cell. (Representing what?) Then there was a massive woman with a towering hat passing along a suburban road, envied by all. (Well?)

Here are the answers : The Strand, Clifford's Inn and Monument. Tom and I had plenty of fun out of that series.

It came to my knowledge that the *News-Chronicle* was looking for a new cartoonist. Such jobs as these are among the plums in the Fleet Street art sphere. I at once told Tom about it, and it was decided that I should see the editor and have some idea of what he was seeking ; which I did.

It was at the time when Mussolini was attacking the Abyssinians with every modern weapon he could produce, including gas, whilst the Abyssinians had little besides archaic rifles and spears. Tom chose this as a subject for a sample cartoon, and produced a brilliant drawing of the Emperor standing in the desert with a few spears lying at his feet. Above, the skies were black with Italian planes.

"Arms, for the love of Allah !" he was crying.

Full of hope, I took it to the *News-Chronicle* and put it before the editor. He looked at it carefully, then gently handed it back to me.

"Yes, very good," he said. "Very good indeed. But don't you know that the Emperor *is a Christian*?"

Sorrowfully I took it back to Cottrell who, like Chevvy Slyme waiting for Montague Tigg, was just round the corner. What he said, I can't repeat, and it was several days before he felt like trying another drawing. By then it was too late. The job was filled.

In Fleet Street mention of "The Morrows" recalls the time when there were four brothers Morrow—all artists. Now Norman and Albert are dead.   George is perhaps the most distinguished humorous artist of his day, and for a number of years was art editor of *Punch*, to which journal he contributed, during much of his life, drawings characterised by a loveable quaintness entirely his own.   No one familiar with *Punch* can be unfamiliar with those mediaeval scenes in which barons and varlets are among the characters ; nor yet with George's odd animals of his own creation.   To look at some of them is to wish such animals really existed.   With them life would never lack laughter.

In person, George might be taken for a rural dean in mufti. Quiet of manner, benign of face, with a wealth of humour in his eyes, he is as modest a master as Fleet Street ever knew.

There was a period when George Morrow's work consisted almost entirely of one full page weekly in *Punch*, while his brother Edwin was contributing lesser illustrated jokes to various papers each week.   At the " Rainbow Tavern " one night, Eddie was introduced to a business man who knew little about artists, but who had seen Eddie's name in some journals.   He was pleased to meet him, and said so.

Presently George entered and joined them at the table, being duly introduced to the business man.

" Really, another Mr. Morrow ? " said the latter, " and do *you* draw, as well as your brother ? "

There was a twinkle in George's eye as he replied : " Not *as well*, perhaps ; *but only once a week.*"

Edwin Morrow possesses an actor's face, and a tragedian's at that, though you cannot listen to him for long without laughing. Many are the stories told of him.   One is of a visit he once paid to an elegant club, the home of big-wigs and high politics. Eddie, notoriously ill-dressed, had some qualms, which were increased when the liveried functionary at the door gave him a supercilious " once-over."   He was admitted, however, and began to feel that he was winning out.   The functionary asked him to follow him up the thickly red-carpeted stairs. Eddie's feeling of inferiority had almost gone by this time.   It might have disappeared altogether had he not passed two super-pompous men on the stairs, and heard one of them say to the other :

" *Of course, they offered me India, but . . .*"

So down went Eddie's confidence again.

Edwin Morrow, by the way, has executed a number of church murals, which have given him a definite status among artists in that kind of work.

Edward Swann, a perfect example of whose work may be found in this book, is another artist with whom I have collaborated. He is a commercial artist of the highest rank, but commerce has not robbed him of any of the temperament attributed to artists. He is still happiest when painting landscapes, or illustrating features such as one I once wrote nightly for the *Star*. Swann did the thumbnail sketches for the feature, which guyed London suburbs in verse, a different suburb each night. I wrote them until I ran out of suburbs. The difficulty with this

The AUTHOR
As caricatured by Ted Davison

feature was to avoid making suburban snobbishness too often the peg, but to get a fresh angle every time. This was a snobbery one about Surbiton :

> " The Resident of Surbiton—
>   (I've lived here all my life, man !)
> Can tolerate the newer folk
>   As little as his wife can.
> His own name being most elite,
>   The reasons for his groans is
> There are two few FitzArbuthnots,
>   And far too many Joneses."

Swann did a snappy little drawing depicting the two types of resident. He excelled, however, with his picture of some typically Arty people, illustrating this one about Hampstead :

" There's a tendency in Hampstead to be ' Arty,'
   For they're learning how to do the Chelsea stuff.
Should you stray into a modern Hampstead party,
   You will very likely find the going rough.
You'll hear hirsute youths and well-begoggled ladies,
   Talking books and pictures you and I think weird,
And although you could not dub them as teetotal,
   You will see how they adore a ginger beard."

Features of this kind are a pleasure to do, especially when one's collaborator is a lively fellow like Edward Swann. For energy, I have rarely met anyone to compare with this juvenile-looking genius. No sooner does he think of an idea than he carries it out. The dissemination of a liking for art is one of Swann's pet activities, and it was he who conceived the idea of the " Artists' Train " which the Southern Railway ran from London to the country each Sunday, conveying artists eager for a real day's sketching. Swann, of course, accompanied them and gave his advice freely to anyone who wanted it. The "Artists' Special " disappeared with the war, but Swann intends to re-start it when better days return.

Edward never fails in repartee. I once introduced him to Squadron-Leader (now Group Captain) Horniman, at that time a well-known " aerobat." Not to be outdone, Swann enthused about his own cousin, who was a wingless accountant (also a Squadron-Leader) at the Air Ministry.

" That's all right, Edward," I said, " but Horniman actually has led squadrons."

" Well, my cousin has lead pencils," came the reply. " So what ? "

Artists, on the whole, are not a provident race, but have a genius for mismanaging their affairs. In consequence, many suffer hardships which might have been avoided ; but they suffer them cheerfully, contriving to extract amusement even from adversity.

There was an artist whom I will call Marley, who was at one time particularly hard-pressed. He was expecting a summons to be served on him at any time. He had sent his wife and family away for an expensive holiday, and he owned a car. Artists are like that. Moreover, he was taking the precaution of not returning home in the evenings until after sunset, when summonses cannot by law be served. One day, however, it became imperative for him to go to his house and collect some drawings, so he took the risk and drove from Fleet Street to the suburb where he lived. There, standing in the roadway before his house, was the sinister figure of one who was unmistakably a bailiff.

" Your name Marley ? " asked the man at the gate.

" No, it isn't," snapped Marley, as he ran up the path and rang his own bell. This he repeated several times with obvious impatience. Then he turned to the bailiff.

" Are *you* waiting for him ? " he asked.

" I certainly am," replied the latter. " This is the third day I've been here. I suppose you want him for the same reason as I do ? "

" That's right," said Marley. " What's *yours* for ? "

" Furniture," growled the bailiff.

" So is mine," said Marley. " Don't think it's much good waiting. Can I give you a lift anywhere ? "

" Well, I'm going back to Town," replied the other, " so if it isn't troubling you——"

" Not at all," said Marley, with as much charm as he could muster. " Jump in."

After a chatty drive into London, the pair parted. Then Marley calmly drove back home to fetch his drawings, the sale of which eventually enabled him to settle the matter.

Another artist I know well, who is now eminent, was once in similar straits, so he retired temporarily to a cottage in the country. He told no one where he was going, but by a little amateur detective work, two friends discovered his whereabouts and called at the cottage one Sunday afternoon. As a joke, they would not give their names to the woman who answered the door, thinking to surprise their friend. He was petrified until he discovered the identity of his callers.

He told the story of his fright to a fellow artist in Fleet Street shortly afterwards. The latter knew that Sunday was a closed day for the " summons hounds," and told him so.

" They can't serve writs or summonses on Sundays, you idiot," he said.

" Perhaps not," agreed the artist, still with a gleam of fear in his eye, " but how did I know they weren't rehearsing for Monday ? "

Sweet are the uses of adversity, Shakespeare tells us, and, so far as the Street is concerned, he is right.   They make men smile.

That able newspaperman, Fred Pullen, of the *Star*, is always ready to tell a story against himself. This one should be told with a Welsh accent on both sides, but until machines print accents they must be imagined.   One of Freddie's early jobs was on a paper in his own country, Wales.   It was in those days when salaries were low, and fifty shillings a week was good pay. One day he was sent to cover a murder trial in the sob-stuff manner. It was his first big assignment, and Freddie put his heart into it. Next day he was called into the proprietor's office.

" Sit down, now, Pullen," he was told with unaccustomed solicitude for his comfort.   " That was a very great story you did for the paper last night.   Great story, indeed.   I gave it to my maids to read, and one of them cried.   Yes, cried."

" Really, sir," said Freddie, " I hope she wasn't very upset."

" I often give stories to my maids to read, Pullen.   It is a great test, indeed," continued the Big Man.   " And to think that one of them cried.   Now, how much are you getting on the paper at present ? "

Freddie, who had heard of Northcliffe doubling salaries at a stroke, replied : " Forty shillings a week, sir."

" Forty shillings a week," repeated the Big Man with deliberation.   " Yes, it was a great story, to make one of my maids cry. And you're getting forty shillings—two pounds—on the paper now ? "

" Yes, sir," said the expectant Pullen.

The Big Man rose to show that the interview was at an end. " I'm gla-ad," he said.

J. T. Bolton was Chairman of the London Press Club for two successive years. This means that J.T.B. is a popular man. Throughout the war he was secretary of *Blighty*, the paper for the Forces. He is a well-known sporting journalist, in which capacity he has met most of the outstanding figures in the sporting world.

During one period he was partly occupied in arranging articles by popular cricketers and footballers for different newspapers. I am not debunking anything when I say that some of these articles needed the expert touch of the practised journalist to make them suitable for publication. In rare cases, he would obtain the information for the article from the sportsman concerned, then prepare the article himself, sending a copy to the former for approval and signature.

This applied especially to one particular idol of the crowd. J.T. would meet him at intervals and obtain material for future articles. He was a man of sparse education, although he knew what views he wanted to express.

For several years, Jimmy Bolton had written the article as required and had sent it, with a cheque, for the signature and approval of the idol of the crowd. On one occasion the I.O.C. gave Jimmy a surprise, for, in returning an article with thanks for the cheque, he said : " Dear Mr. Bolton, I reckon this is the best article I've ever wrote."

One of the questions which, sooner or later, the layman asks the journalist is : " Do you know Nathaniel Gubbins ? "

Personally, I have known Nat Gubbins for many years—even before he began his famous feature, " Sitting On The Fence," in the *Sunday Express*. I well remember the trepidation with which he embarked on a column destined to make him the most outstanding humorous writer of his day. He talked to me about it shortly before it appeared, wondering if it would be a flop. Even the title, now a Sunday morning institution, is indicative of the doubting mood in which he started the feature. He did not know which way he was going to jump.

John Gordon, trenchant editor of the *Sunday Express*, once told me the story of how " Sitting On The Fence" came into being. It happened when J.G. was planning to make Page Three an entirely distinctive part of the paper. Hitherto news had been carried over to it from Page Two, but this was now to cease, and the page was to be devoted to " regular " features to which readers would look forward week by week. Already there were appearing on the page Lord Castlerosse, James Douglas, and, I think, Ripley. But there was no feature of a really light kind.

It chanced that at that time Gordon went to a party in the West End, given to a departing member of the staff. The after-dinner hit was the reading of a number of "cod" telegrams, purporting to come from "conspicuous absentees." These were so funny that J.G. made inquiries as to who was responsible for them, and was told that one of his reporters, by name of Gubbins, had written them. John knew him as a shy young man, and was mildly surprised.

Then came another dinner, with the advertisement manager, L. W. Needham, in the chair. And again appeared another series of subtly humorous telegrams, which, as before, Gordon traced to the retiring young reporter.

Next day J.G. sent for Nat Gubbins and asked him if he would undertake a weekly humorous feature, whereupon Nat said that that was exactly what he had always wanted to do. So it was arranged that he should write it, Gordon promising to give it an eight weeks' run so that Gubbins could "find his feet." And so the feature started. There also started a series of abusive letters from readers, complaining of having such nonsense being put before them. Even high members of the *Express* had unpleasant things to say about it. J.G. did not feel too happy about it, but was determined to let "Sitting On The Fence" have its eight weeks' run.

Then one day he found Lord Beaverbrook chuckling over it. It was really good, said his Lordship. John told him of the dubious reception it had had, whereupon "The Beaver," as he is familiarly called in Fleet Street, exclaimed :

"But surely you're not thinking of stopping it?"

"I'm certainly not," replied Gordon. Nor did he, and so the feature continued.

When, early in the war, Nat Gubbins was taken ill, Gordon was in a fix, for the illness promised to be a long one. Rather than suspend the feature, Gordon himself went through the early files and composed "Sitting on the Fence" from old matter for five or six weeks. To his astonishment, he received letters, some from readers who had previously reviled that very material, saying that Gubbins was getting better every week! The only complaint came from Nat on his sick bed, pleading that it should be stated that it was old matter. But Gordon knew better than that !

When I last saw J.G. he told me that he considers his discovery of Nathaniel Gubbins to be the outstanding success of his career.

Those who expect to find in Gubbins a genial, joking humorist are disappointed. They meet instead a quiet, rather gloomy-looking man with the wandering eyes of a dreamer. This is explained by the fact that Nathaniel Gubbins is not primarily a humorist at all ; he uses humour as a medium for satire.

I once made the mistake of saying to him that some particular part of his last Sunday's column was specially funny. Nat turned a slightly baleful eye upon me and said :

" I'm *never* funny."

That is partly the case, as an analysis of " Sitting On the Fence " will show. When he wrote " In a Safe Hotel," you could read his intense contempt for the people he epitomised in the wealthy woman and her companion, evacuated to a safe hotel.

" The only way to see this war through," he made the elder woman say, " is to keep calm and carry on as though nothing unusual is taking place. What's for dinner ? "

That amusing character, " The Sparrow," who periodically flies away from his wife to visit " The Other Sparrow " or the Tree-tops Club, is nothing if not a caustic pointer at the domesticated woman who overdoes it.

In " The Diary of a Worm " you see the hen-pecking wife with piffling suburban ideas of respectability, jealous of the wives of more successful men than her husband, who is just a natural little fellow, liking his glass at the local and doing his best.

Of course, not all of " Sitting On the Fence " is satire. Gubbins knows how much powder he can mix with the jam.

His humour in conversation is unaccompanied by the advertise-ment of a smile. I met him one morning coming to Fleet Street from his home in Surrey. His children were young at the time, and he told me how, on the previous Saturday, he had engaged a room as a kind of office nearby, where he could work undisturbed. On the Monday morning, he discovered what the Saturday afternoon had not shown him—that there was a saw-mill adjacent, with a circular saw which positively seared his brain.

" I'm giving it up," he said moodily. " You *can* sock the kids, but you can't sock a circular saw."

Once Gubbins surprised his readers by printing a serious poem in his column. It was a tribute to Kitty, Fleet Street's familiar flower-girl, who, during the heavy blitzes, continued her rounds of the taverns with her basket of flowers. Few men with a woman companion would fail to respond to this expert but lovable saleswoman's " Flowers for your lady, sir ? " This is what Gubbins wrote :

> " In the autumn gladiolas,
> In the spring the daffodils,
> Winter asters, summer roses,
> Heather from the Scottish hills ;
> Kitty took them in her basket
> Round the taverns of the town
> (' A bunch of flowers for your lady ? ')
> While the bombs were dropping down.
>
> Red and white and pink carnations,
> Marigold and mignonette,
> Peony and polyanthus,
> Sweet William and sweet violet.
> Kitty hawked them round the taverns,
> ' Thank you, dear, a drop of gin.
> (A bunch of flowers for your lady ?)
> There them sirens go agin.'
>
> In her basket there were lilies,
> Golden Rod and London Pride,
> Canterbury Bells and tulips,
> Poppies washed by wind and tide.
> Kitty hawked them round the taverns,
> Round the taverns of the town
> (' A bunch of flowers for your lady ? ')
> While the bombs were dropping down."

There you have a side to Nathaniel Gubbins' nature to say nothing of his poetic talent, which hitherto most had suspected, but few encountered.

CHAPTER VII

FLEET STREET IN STONE

No London street is so rich in history as this third of a mile between Temple Bar and Ludgate Circus. Not a yard of it but has some story to tell ; not one of the narrow courts which lead off it but has been trodden by the feet of the famous.

Rogues found sanctuary in the purlieus of the White Friars' monastery, in Hanging Sword Alley and thereabouts. Gibbets stood at the lane-ends of Fleet Street, and the groans of dying men were heard where to-day the presses roar.

A cavalcade of great literary men passes across the page of Fleet Street history — Milton, who lived there—Pepys, born there — Dr. Samuel Johnson, whose shrine it still is — Goldsmith, with his debts and domiciles round about — Izaac Walton, with his shop near St. Dunstan's. All these and many more belonged to Fleet Street.

The grisly hand of the Plague was laid about it, and it was licked by the flames of the Great Fire—the latter a presage of the devastation to come, by design and not by accident, when civilisation had reached the year of 1940.

"THE DOCTOR"
After Joshua Reynolds' portrait

Fleet Street can claim four churches, only one of which, St. Dunstan's-in-the-West, is actually on the Street itself. The others lie nearby to the north and south. They are the Temple Church, St. Bride's and St. Andrew's. Of three of these four churches a friend of mine, E. F. P. Bartlett, wrote the following quaint verses in the *Daily Express* :

" Three Saints in their churches keep watch over Fleet Street,
   St. Bride to the South and St. Andrew to North,
While honest St. Dunstan he sits by the Temple
   And sees all the paper vans run to and forth.

Says St. Bride to St. Dunstan : ' Oh, what is the uproar ?
   I'm all of a tremble from steeple to pews.'
He says, ' My dear Bridget, I pray you, don't fidget ;
   They're printing the papers to tell you the news.'

Three Saints in their churches keep watch over Fleet Street
   With presses a-roaring on every side,
So pray for the people who bring out the papers,
   Oh, Holy St. Andrew, St. Dunstan, St. Bride."

Bartlett's use of the name Bridget was apt, for St. Bride's was originally St. Bridget's, named after a sixth century Irish saint, who, it was said, was buried in the same grave as St. Patrick.

Mention of St. Bride's goes back as far as 1222, although the church must have been built long before then.   In the reign of Charles I it was considerably repaired, only to be totally destroyed by the Great Fire of London in 1666.   Soon after that, Sir Christopher Wren came upon the scene and built the new church. At first it had only a tower, but in 1701, a year before Queen Anne's accession, there was added the famous spire which now adorns it. An impression by that versatile Fleet Street artist, Will Farrow, accompanies this chapter.

After St. Paul's, St. Bride's is considered by many to be Wren's masterpiece.   The steeple rises from the tower in four graceful tapering, octagonal storeys and is certainly " one of the sights " of Fleet Street, indeed of London.   Of the interior, A. E. Daniell, in his book " London City Churches " wrote :

" St. Bride's, with its panelled walls, its pews, and its galleries overhead, has a peaceful, old-world aspect, which is delightfully soothing when one passes from the turmoil of Fleet Street into the quietude of the sacred building.   It is pervaded by an unquestionable charm—but a charm which is rather to be felt than to be described."

Alas for its charm !   On the night of the Great Blitz, when much

"THE JOURNALISTS'
CATHEDRAL"
The shell of blitzed St. Bride's
Church

WILL FARROW
draws Wren's famous steeple
from an unusual angle

of the City was in flames, incendiaries fell on the church of St. Bride and turned it into a furnace. Fire belched from its roof and its beautiful round and oval windows, while flames licked their way into the belfry. The famous peal of twelve bells, whose music had rejoiced the hearts of Londoners for so long, came crashing down to become great pieces of broken metal at the foot of the tower.

With several other newspapermen, I stood and looked at these mute evidences of former glory on the morning after, while smoke and steam were still rising from the nave. Fleet Street men are hard-bitten enough, but this hurt us inconceivably, for was not St. Bride's Our Church, and had it not come to be known as " The Journalists' Cathedral " ? Had we not stood in those mellowed pews at memorial services to our friends, and had we not turned into St. Bride's, a little self-consciously perhaps, from the turbulence of the Street, for odd moments of meditation ?

Passing into Fleet Street, I encountered Charlie Sutton, then foreign editor of the *Daily Express*. Charles was gazing up at the hollow steeple, from which even now there floated sad little wisps of smoke. As there is a song which insists that " smoke gets in your eyes " I must assume that the moistness in Sutton's had that practical explanation. We turned into " Poppin's " nearby and ordered whiskies . . .

But Wren built well, and, although everything perishable in the building had gone, the stone-work still stood, although badly burnt by the intense heat. The pillars have now been encased in concrete for support, so perhaps the day may come when we may meditate again in the " Journalists' Cathedral."

So went one of Bartlett's " three saints." That night also the church of St. Andrew was gutted, together with its neighbour, the City Temple of renown. This church of St. Andrew is not, by some few hundred yards, *in* Fleet Street, but its gaunt shell overshadows the *Evening Standard* in Shoe Lane and the ruins of the *Morning Advertiser* which was blitzed on the same night.

Here is a church whose earliest traced history takes us back to the year 971, according to a charter in the reign of King Edgar. In the fourteenth century, its advowson was passed into the hands of the abbot and monks of Bermondsey. With them it remained until the convent's dissolution by Henry VIII. (It is interesting to note that many of the City's churches belonged to monasteries until their dissolution. St. Bride's, for instance, was in the hands of the Abbot and Convent of Westminster.)

St. Andrew's was rebuilt in the fifteenth century, but in the centuries which followed, it fell into a state of general dilapidation until it was reconstructed by Wren. It was not one of the " Great Fire " churches, for it was missed by that conflagration. Even as it stands, it is not exactly a " Wren Church," for Wren left the tower much as he found it and devoted himself to reconstructing the body. Like the other Fleet Street churches, St. Andrew's provides many literary memories, an amusing one being of Charles Lamb, who acted as best man at William Hazlitt's wedding there. Some years later, Lamb wrote a letter to Southey in which he said :

" I am going to stand godfather ; I don't like the business. I cannot muster up decorum for these occasions ; I shall certainly disgrace the font. I was at Hazlitt's marriage, and had liked to have been turned out several times during the ceremony. Anything awful makes me laugh. I once misbehaved at a funeral. Yet I can read about these ceremonies with pious and proper feelings. The realities of life only seem its mockeries."

In the register of St. Andrew's was entered the interment of the young poet Chatterton, who became famous before he committed suicide at the age of eighteen—in a garret. It is recorded that he was buried in the Shoe Lane Workhouse Burial-ground, close to where the Farringdon Market stands to-day. This was in 1770. Thus the poetry of this unhappy boy has survived for the best part of two centuries.

Chatterton was not the only tragic poet whose history lingers around a Fleet Street church. There was Richard Lovelace, that ill-starred Royalist poet, who, having spent his fortune in the King's cause and, having been imprisoned twice for that same cause, died in squalor in Gunpowder Alley by Fleet Street (blitzed 1941). He was buried in St. Bride's Church, though in what circumstances it is difficult to ascertain. It was during his imprisonment in Westminster Gatehouse that he wrote his undying little poem : " To Althea from Prison," which ended :

> " Stone walls do not a prison make,
>   Nor iron bars a cage ;
> Minds innocent and quiet take
>   That for a hermitage ;
> If I have freedom in my love,
>   And in my soul am free,
> Angels alone that soar above
>   Enjoy such liberty."

Comparable with this was the poem he wrote when setting forth in support of his sovereign's arms—" To Lucasta on Going to the Wars." It began :

> " Tell me not, sweet, I am unkind,
>   That from the nunnery
> Of thy chaste breast and quiet mind
>   To war and arms I fly."

It ended thus :

> " I could not love thee, dear, so much,
>   Loved I not honour more. "

Lovelace was contemporary with Milton, who for a time lived at a tailor's house in St. Bride's Churchyard. One imagines that the two must often have met ; one may further imagine, too fondly, perhaps, that Milton may have been behind the choice of Lovelace's last resting place, and that, but for him, the bones of the destitute Cavalier poet might have been laid in some less distinguished place. I must admit, however, that this theory is purely my own.

Of the four churches mentioned at the beginning of this chapter, a third was destroyed by enemy action—the Temple Church, which is unique among English churches in that it was the church of the Knights Templars. Norman in origin, it possesses a perfect vaulted porch which leads into the Round. This latter is the original church and is circular in construction, so exquisite in its architecture and ornamentation that there is probably no church in the country which can vie with it. Here lie—or did lie—the effigies of warriors, with their legs crossed, commonly supposed to be an indication that these were Knights who took part in the Crusades.

The Oblong, which adjoins the Round, was built a century or so later than the latter, which was dedicated in 1185. Alas, the whole church was gutted, but it has received similar treatment to that given to St. Bride's, and may eventually be restored. Fascinating as this church is, it cannot really be claimed as a Fleet Street church, since it belongs exclusively to the lawyers' domain—the Temple, that sequestered area whose courts, halls, squares and chambers fared even worse in the blitz than did the church, which was built of sounder stuff.

We will therefore turn to " Honest St. Dunstan."

St. Dunstan's-in-the-West, so named to distinguish it from St. Dunstan's-in-the-East at the other end of the City, was, like St. Bride's, at one time in the hands of the Westminster monastery. Unlike St. Bride's, it remains comparatively intact, although it narrowly escaped destruction in the unexpected incendiary raid early in 1944, when the bombs spattered down upon the Strand end of Fleet Street, turning midnight into phosphorescent noon. I was working late (beginning this book) in the vicinity, and was just writing about St. Dunstan's lantern tower, when I heard the cry :

" St. Dunstan's is on fire ! "

Sure enough it was. Incendiaries had lodged among the beams at the top of the tower, which was well alight. A lantern tower it indeed was, in that exciting hour. The intense light within threw into beautiful relief the filigree through which the setting sun had shone not many hours before. At least a dozen fire-engines had arrived on the spot, for other buildings nearby were spurting flames. Presently a water-tower shot up to its full height with a fireman perched perilously at the top. It did not reach the full height of the church tower, which is 130 feet, but it was sufficiently high for the intrepid fireman to turn his powerful hose on to the blazing tower. Thus we watched with relief the saving of St. Dunstan's.

A wedding had been arranged to take place in the church on the following day, and the rector, Dr. MacDonald, undaunted by the ordeal of the previous night, went through with it, and the couple were married among the masses of charred debris which had crashed from the tower into the body of the church itself.

Providence has apparently shown much mercy to St. Dunstan's for it escaped but narrowly from the Great Fire which destroyed buildings only a few doors away.

The present church is modern as City churches go, for the old church was pulled down in 1829 and the present one built on its site. Its octagonal interior still carries on its walls a number of the monuments which existed in the old church, so that the visitor is apt to believe that the church is older than it really is. One of these monuments, in the form of a plain tablet, is to the memory of a lawyer who died twenty years before the old church was taken down. Here it is :

> " To the Memory
> of Hobson Judkin, Esq.
> late of Clifford's Inn
> The Honest Solicitor
> who departed this life June the 30 1812
>
> ———————
>
> This Tablet was erected by his clients
> as a token of gratitude and respect for his
> honest, faithful and friendly Conduct to them
> thro' Life.
> Go Reader and imitate
> Hobson Judkin."

The south exterior wall of St. Dunstan's has several claims upon the passer-by's attention in normal times. During the war the stone statue of Queen Elizabeth (circa 1580) was walled up, as was also the fine bronze bust of Lord Northcliffe, as a precaution against enemy action. There was to be seen, however, a most remarkable—indeed, spectacular—clock, in which two great giants, " clad in loin cloths and of ferocious aspect," strike the hours with their clubs upon a bell, to the constant interest of strangers.

This clock was set up soon after the Great Fire, and remained until the old church was pulled down in 1829, when it disappeared from Fleet Street for about a century ; but let me draw upon the late Walter George Bell, the great historian of Fleet Street, for the story of the disappearance of these two automata.

" The third Marquis of Hertford, when a small and impressionable boy, was taken to see the clock at St. Dunstan's Church. His delight in the working figures inspired visions of the joy of ultimate possession, and he declared : ' When I am a man I will buy that clock, and put it in my house.' Early last century Marylebone Park became converted into Regent's Park, and the Crown reserved portions of the land for terrace-houses and villas. A site of six acres was taken on lease by Lord Hertford, who built a villa there. It happened that this very year, 1830, old St. Dunstan's Church in Fleet Street was coming down for rebuilding, and in the new plan, which placed the church farther back and allowed for a considerable widening of the old highway, the clock and giants had no part.

" Lord Hertford, then grown a man, seized the opportunity to fulfil his boyish wish. For the clock, the bells, the club-bearing giants, and the storey in which they were framed, . . . he offered 200 guineas. That sum was accepted and the trophies were carted to Regent's Park."

Mr. Walter Bell, who died but a few years ago, also described how he made a visit to the giants in his own time :

" The Earl of Londesborough, their present custodian, kindly gave me leave to inspect the giants at St. Dunstan's, Regent's Park, his town house ; and there, like any of the gaping sight-seers of generations long since dead, and gone, who have stopped in the Street to watch their antics, I stood before these time-honoured relics, which in their day had been a cause of wonderment to young and old. With the dial projecting over the gravelled path, the frame of masonry containing the giants and the bells has been rebuilt on the garden front, just as it was in the old church, and as the sun goes his daily round, still the clubs beat the hours and quarter hours."

How comes it to be, then, that to-day the giants are back again at St. Dunstan's-in-the-West, doing their performance as of old to the amusement of the passers-by in Fleet Street ?

The giants are back through the generosity of the late Lord Rothermere, who bought the house in Regent's Park and transferred the clock to its original home.

In the middle of the seventeenth century, a few doors from St. Dunstan's, a mild-mannered, middle-aged man kept a shirt-shop. There was nothing much to mark him from the ordinary tradesman, but if you look at a tablet on the south wall of St. Dunstan's, you will see that his name was Izaac Walton.

The tablet was erected by anglers, whose fraternity look upon him almost as a patron saint. Although his " The Compleat Angler " was published as long ago as 1653, it remains with us still, the perfect companion for the quiet mind. It was some years after his retirement that Walton turned to writing, and produced, in addition to his masterpiece, a number of " lives," embracing Dr. Donne, George Herbert and others. But it is as the author of " The Compleat Angler " that he is best remembered and loved, and it seems fitting that his book should have been published by " Richard Marriot in St. Dunstan's Churchyard, Flete-street."

Within the church you may sit and meditate upon a stained glass window placed there in honour of the Gentle Angler, a kindly man and his neighbour's friend.

*   *   *

It has not been the happiest of tasks to treat our churches thus scantily, so redolent with history are they, and so varied a picture of Fleet Street through the ages do they present. I would have liked to delve into their parish registers and, say, into the ward-mote register of St. Dunstan's, where one may find such intriguing entries as the following :

> " We present James Walmsley and William Summers for annoying of divers inhabitants of Fleet Street, and the Whyte-fryars by killing dogges for hawkes, and also keeping them long alyve howling and crying, and after they have kill'd them, theyr blood and filthe groeth soe noysome that yt will be very dangerous for infection yf yt be suffered."

But, no, I will not be tempted. Hawks or no hawks in 1640 Fleet Street ! We have news-hawks now.

*   *   *

Mention of " Whyte-fryars " brings us to the area about

Whitefriars Street which runs from Fleet Street towards the Embankment. Here it was that the Carmelite friars settled in the thirteenth century. Their habit actually was brown, but they derived their name owing to their wearing a white mantle over their habit on frequent occasions. Then there is Carmelite Street just by, and Carmelite House, the first home of the *Daily Mail* and still that of the *Evening News*.

This area, which later came to be called Alsatia, developed into a sanctuary for evildoers. Indeed, after the dissolution it became a veritable kingdom of crime on its own. Until the suppression of the monasteries by Henry VIII, sanctuary was a tacitly understood thing, with inclusions and exclusions of different offences to which it was normally granted. The period of sanctuary was forty days, which gave the unfortunate one time to make some defence, to make personal arrangements or, in some cases, to make his " get-away."

But with the dissolution of the monasteries, the sanctuary afforded by the Carmelite friars automatically disappeared. Even the friars themselves were more or less outlaws. It was then that the " kingdom " of Alsatia came into existence, and a self-made sanctuary was instituted by every class of evildoer it is possible to imagine. Hitherto, highway robbery and the like were excluded from sanctuary, but, with the disappearance of monkish authority, the perpetrators of crimes, however grisly, claimed the immunity of Alsatia.

The wrongdoers had at least one legal point in their favour. The ground which they had chosen for their own had been consecrated for religious use, and, though it was in the City of London, the Lord Mayor had no power over it. Nor, apparently, had anyone else ! Many were the scrimmages which took place in those narrow courts between the sheriff's men and the loose livers of Alsatia. I cannot do better here than quote Macaulay :

" Insolvents were to be found in every dwelling from cellar to garret. Of these, a large proportion were knaves and libertines, and were followed to their asylum by women more abandoned than themselves. The civil power was unable to keep order in a district swarming with such inhabitants ; and thus Whitefriars became the favourite resort of all who wished to be emancipated from the restraints of the law. Though these immunities legally belonging to the place extended only to cases of debt — cheats, false witnesses, forgers and highwaymen found refuge there. For amidst a rabble so desperate, no police officer's life was in safety. At the cry of " Rescue," bullies with swords and cudgels, and termagant hags with spits and broomsticks, poured forth by hundreds ; and the intruder was fortunate if he escaped back into Fleet Street, hustled, stripped and jumped upon. Even the warrant of the Lord Chief Justice of England could not be executed without the help of a company of musketeers."

Alsatia was vague in its boundaries, for they were made often enough to suit the needs of its inhabitants. In those days the Thames came up nearly to its southern border, and thus afforded one more means of dodging the authorities. To the west lay the Temple, and the Alsatians claimed that the area about the Temple Church was a sanctuary by right. But they were up against the lawyers in this respect, who built brick barricades to keep out the unsavoury mob. Nevertheless, there were many pitched battles between the latter and the " young gentlemen of the Law." The only real boundary seemed to be Fleet Street itself, which runs at right angles to Whitefriars Street, then the centre of Alsatian lawlessness.

Anyone knowing the intricacies of courts, alleys and streets which, even to-day, criss-cross the area between Fleet Street and the Thames, will appreciate the difficulties of those who tried to impose the law upon those who lived there. Moreover, the taverns and low houses were all conveniently fitted with alternative exits, so that when the sheriff's men entered by one door, the malefactors nipped out of the other, after which one might have sought them on the Thames, in the Temple or anywhere else with equal chance of failure.

Perhaps the most pestilential part of Alsatia was Ram Alley, now called Hare Place, though why such an historic name should have been changed, heaven knows. Hare Place to-day is the little alley which runs from Fleet Street by the side of " El Vino " wine house into the blitzed waste which lies immediately behind it. I believe there was a board to indicate that this was the site of Ram Alley, and that it was lost in the devastation.

Wrote Mr. Walter Bell of Ram Alley : " Everything known of Ram Alley pictures it in a condition of decay, which seemed to have been its unchanging state. A glimpse into the alley from Fleet Street disclosed a line of dilapidated house-fronts. Broken gutters, which no one troubled to repair, delivered a shower-bath upon the passer-by after every rainstorm. Over the shops, with their clatter and smell, were quiet rooms, whence came occasionally the sound of riot and disorder, and faces peered out of the patched windows. They were not pleasant faces. The ' widdys ' who figure so frequently in Ram Alley's scandalous annals were widows only by courtesy.

" It was the custom of the inhabitants to fling their refuse into a laystall, or heap, before their houses. When it became too offensive even for them, they swept it surreptitiously into Fleet Street, and thus were at constant warfare with constituted authority."

Yes, you who take your wine in the sequestered back room of " El Vino " to-day, may find it interesting to meditate upon the strange history of that spot.

Another Alsatian bolt-hole, which could well have been called ripe, was Hanging Sword Alley which exists to-day, and under its own name withal. You enter the narrow alley on the left of the top of Whitefriars Street, where you turn right and follow it parallel-wise until you emerge via some steep steps into the bottom of the same street. It is flanked to-day by the backs of more modern buildings, but its narrowness remains the same.

The alley's name is not so sinister as it may seem, for it came from a house which carried the sign of a hanging sword, it being the custom in those days for many houses to have their own sign. Be that as it may, the place had a foul reputation, not improved by the presence in it of a house called the Blood Bowl, said to have been the scene of various murders. Hogarth depicted it in one of his grimmest prints, showing a body being heaved through a trap door in the floor.

To walk down Hanging Sword Alley by night, even nowadays, is often to catch a mental whiff of the old Alsatia, for you may frequently see vagabonds, with their unsavoury bags of belongings, asleep in its murky doorways. From my own observation these are often the same men, night after night. Unwittingly they have chosen for themselves a sanctuary older than they could ever suppose. *** * *

Little courts and alleys run right and left from Fleet Street like bones from a herring's spine, and each one leads into a maze of further courts which lie behind " The Street " to north and south.   At least they *did* lie behind it until the 1941 Blitz which, alas, obliterated so many of them that it is difficult to-day to say accurately just where they ran.   Gone Pemberton Row ; gone Neville's Court, where once Handel lived.   Gone Gunpowder Alley, where Lovelace spent his last unhappy days.

Yet the stranger is apt to say that Fleet Street escaped the Blitz. This is true of the street itself, which runs like a ribbon between the dead labyrinths which lie either side of it, but you have to take only a hundred steps to the north or south to find areas inhabited solely by the ghosts of a rich past.

Most of the courts which lead from Fleet Street to these historic vacancies have romantic names.   Here are a few of them : Poppin's Court, so named after a building which had the " Popyngay " for its sign ; Salisbury Court, where once stood the town house and garden of the Bishops of Salisbury ; Wine Office Court, a name that speaks for itself ; Lombard Alley, which does the same ; Mitre Court, which ran beside the old Mitre Tavern ; Johnson's Court, named, not after the Doctor as the fond would believe, but because a wealthy Elizabethan citizen lived there.   Mark you, these by no means exhaust the list ; and each has its history and its traditions of the great men who once trod their narrow ways.

Here and there in Fleet Street you come across a plaque telling you a little of the building's history.   There are thus indicated the sites of the Devil Tavern, where Child's Bank now stands. This famous tavern is known to have existed early in the sixteenth century, and stood until it was pulled down to make room for an extension of the bank in 1778.   Originally the sign proclaimed the tavern to be " The Devil and St. Dunstan."   The board was " painted with a vigorous representation of St. Dunstan, the patron of the goldsmith's art, and his sable majesty leering over his shoulder, tempting him from his labours at the forge."

Almost opposite the " Devil " stood another famous old tavern, the " King's Head," which dated back to 1291.   A plaque near the bottom of Chancery Lane now marks its site.   The tavern figures largely in political history, for it was a meeting place of various factions, and it is said that at least one rebellion was hatched there. There is also evidence of its being highly decorated on an occasion when Queen Elizabeth passed down Fleet Street in state.

It was also a bank—Hoare's—which engulfed another tavern, the " Mitre," a regular haunt of Dr. Johnson and his companions. A plaque marks the site. The " Mitre " stood alongside the notorious Ram Alley, to which I have referred, and, as it had an exit to that unsavoury court, it was well used by the gentry of Alsatia. Just behind the site of the old " Mitre " stands to-day a more recent " Mitre," an interesting place generally known as the " Clachan," where many Scottish tartans adorn the walls. Because of its proximity to its predecessor, it has been credited with Johnsonian associations. It is certainly a very old building, as its stone cellars show, so that if it were a coffee-house in Johnson's day, as is suggested, there is quite a possibility that it was a calling-place of the old autocrat. My belief in this is heightened by the one-time presence in the bar of a bust of the Doctor.

This bust was a particular fancy of mine, and it did more to reincarnate the old boy in my mind than any legend has ever done. Lately, I have learnt that it was a cast of Nollekens' bust, and therefore an authentic portrait. Once, no doubt, it was white, but years of frowning through a tobacco-laden haze had given it the appearance of well-smoked meerschaum.

" One morn I missed him from th' accustomed spot," and I learnt with some grief that a barmaid, during dusting operations, had dropped him on the floor, from which only a brush and dustpan could retrieve him.

On the wall of the *Nottingham Guardian* London office, at the corner of Bouverie Street and Fleet Street, is a plaque telling us that here lived Thomas Tompion, " The Father of English Clock-making," at the turn of the seventeenth and eighteenth centuries. He was buried, it says, in Westminster Abbey. Thomas Tompion was, without doubt, the most celebrated clock-maker whom England has produced, and examples of his work fetch high prices to-day. One of these is a clock made for William III, which is now in a private collection. It needs winding only once a year, and still keeps perfect time.

Salisbury Court, however, displays the most interesting plaque of all, for it denotes that Samuel Pepys, diarist, was born there. Pepys, a regular playgoer, as his Diary so vividly shows, was familiar with the Salisbury Court Playhouse which he frequently attended. It was here that he witnessed a first performance by one of the Elizabethan dramatists.

" Sep 9 : To Salisbury Court Playhouse, where was acted the first time ' Tis Pity She's a Whore ', a simple play, and ill-acted, only it was my fortune to sit by a most pretty and ingenious lady, which pleased me much."

So wrote the old rascal in his Diary.

Fleet Street has its own verse about Pepys, reputedly " made on the premises," which runs, so far as I can remember it, as follows. (Having forgotten the name of the discoverer of the new pronunciation, I have called him Nesfield.)

> " Some people there are, I believe there are heaps,
>   Who always refer to the Diarist as *Peeps*.
>   But some, so precise and pedantic their step is,
>   Always refer to old Samuel as *Peppys*.
>   But those who are right, and I follow their steps,
>   Whenever they speak of him always say *Pepps*.
>   Yet Nesfield avers that the truth still escapes,
>   For *Peeps* isn't *Peppys*, nor *Pepps* ; it is *Papes*."

Commit that to memory and you've acquired a literary parlour-trick.

CHAPTER VIII.

CHESTERTON NIGHTS.

IT was my good fortune at one period to know the Chestertons well—Mrs. Cecil Chesterton and her brother-in-law, G. K. Chesterton. Mrs. Cecil—Keith, as we called her—was married to G.K.'s brilliant brother Cecil, who died in the last war on the brink of a future which undoubtedly would have transcended his present—and he was already a famous man.

Mrs. Cecil Chesterton, when I first met her, lived in the only flat actually in Fleet Street, at No. 3, near Temple Bar at the Strand end of the Street. She is one of the cleverest and most sincere women I have ever met, but when she moved from the flat, her appearances in Fleet Street became less and less frequent. Until then, it was something of an honour to belong to her circle which included many outstanding people in the literary world, including, needless to say, the great G.K. himself.

Keith does not suffer fools gladly. She either likes you or does not. No one is left in doubt for long. The consequence was that the gatherings at No. 3 were what you might call hand-picked.

I first met Mrs. Chesterton when her sympathies were moving strongly in defence of the down-and-out women of London. There was a tendency then, and always had been, to overlook the plight of the destitute woman, and for the authorities and sociologists to think the world of the under-dog was inhabited by men alone. Actually the number of women struggling in the sediment of London humanity was far more than London had conceived, or cared to conceive, and it took Mrs. Cecil Chesterton to discover this.

Except for her novels, which she had written before her marriage under the name of John K. Prothero, all her work was activated by her sympathies. But the culmination came with her fight for down-and-out women which ended in the establishment of the Cecil Houses, which accepted outcasts without expecting a certificate of chastity which most of the charitable institutions seemed to require, without probing into their pasts and without insulting them into the bargain.

Keith discussed the matter with me, saying that she proposed to put the matter to a personal test. She would go to one of the big railway termini round about midnight without any money, say she had come to London to look for a job but had lost the few shillings she had on the journey, and see what happened to her.

This may not sound a very arduous undertaking, but it must be remembered that Mrs. Chesterton had pledged herself to spend at least a fortnight, from that night onwards, as a destitute woman, not to return to her flat in the meantime, and to accept no outside help from those who knew her. Add to this the fact that it was winter, and you will have some idea of the ordeal which she had set herself.

There was nothing robust about her. She was not " tough," to outward appearances, anyway, and she was as fond of the good things of life as anyone. I have heard her described as a " wisp of a woman " which is a good, if trite, description. But the " wisp " is made of sterner stuff than many would imagine, and a look into her eyes will hint at a strong will behind them.

We arranged that she should write a series of articles on her experiences for the *Sunday Express*, and that I, in my capacity as a feature agent, should handle the matter. This meant meeting her to get her weekly copy, often written in distressing circumstances, arranging for photographs of her " in action," and so on. These articles she later supplemented and wrote a book called " Darkest London," to which I must refer readers who wish to read the full story of this courageous experiment, with all its sociological implications.

So it happened that one miserable night, a few of us had a farewell drink with her, then said good-bye to a drab little figure with nothing in her pocket but the bus fare to the terminus she had chosen. Under her arm she carried a shabby parcel containing a few belongings ; in her heart, the will to see it through.

She found the situation facing a destitute woman much worse than she imagined, and her book relentlessly exposes the nature of her reception at various hostels, the insulting questions she was asked, the assumption of her as a bad character, the work she was put to do and the food she was made to eat. On the other hand, Keith was ready to give full credit to the places which treated her as an honest human being, down on her luck. In particular, she praised the helpfulness and broad-mindedness of the London " Coppers."

It must not be overlooked that all this happened a number of years ago and that numerous improvements have been introduced since then. Nevertheless, it was Mrs. Chesterton who brought to light the need of more assistance for the under-woman, and no doubt her establishment of the Cecil Houses set an example which fortunately has been followed.

At one point during her experiment, Keith was reduced to selling matches in the street—*actually* reduced, for to the end she refused any help not within the reach of the genuine case. It was at this point that I once had to meet her on a rainy night. She had telephoned her locality, and I found her at a street corner near Piccadilly Circus, wet through and with a raging cold. I tried to persuade her that she was taking a great risk, that she had already been at it long enough to justify her articles, her book and her conscience, but she refused to be taken back to her flat or into a restaurant for a square meal. I did, however, almost by force, take her into the four-ale end of a nearby pub and give her a good shot of brandy.

The energy with which she set about creating the Cecil Houses afterwards was amazing. She even persuaded Bernard Shaw to give his support in person. This was at a meeting she held one afternoon in a West End theatre, the stalls of which were filled with an interested audience. On the stage were Bernard Shaw, Sir Gerald du Maurier, the then Lady Diana Manners, Lady Bertha Dawkins (a Lady-in-Waiting to Queen Mary, thus signifying Her Majesty's support) and a number of others from Debrett and Who's Who.

It was one of Shaw's principles not to give to organised charity—not noticeably, anyhow—and it was amusing to watch Sir Gerald du Maurier trying all his arts to cajole a subscription out of him. There was a collection taken, but, in addition, Sir Gerald appealed for substantial donations from the richer ones in the theatre. This brought promises of cheques from a number of people, but not from Mr. Shaw. In vain did Sir Gerald coax him as one might a recalcitrant dog, even to the point of patting him, but Shaw was obdurate. Nevertheless, a mysterious cheque eventually found its way into the funds.

The evenings at No. 3 Fleet Street provided a good deal of fun, particularly when Keith suggested that we should give a Fleet Street play for Fleet Street people. The idea was to be based on the peasant plays of Austria, or somewhere, in which there were no written lines, only a theme—you could scarcely call it a plot—which was the basis of extempore dialogue among the actors.

W. R. Titterton, then editing " G. K.'s Weekly," produced a theme for a play called " St. Vanglia : The Witch of Fleet Street," which guyed the Street of Ink unmercifully. The rehearsals were always accompanied by plenty of " lotion," each bringing a bottle of something, but since, at each rehearsal, everyone said something different from what they had said at the previous one, we found ourselves on The Night almost without any prearranged dialogue.

We called ourselves " The Peasant Players of Fleet Street," which sounds " precious," though we were nothing of the kind. We had no scenery and no costumes, other than odds and ends which each individual raked up, yet the play received such a Press as would have put any West End show on its feet for a year. It was given at the Inns of Court Hall, and admission was by invitation only, with the exception of a hundred or so who got wind of it and came in.

St. Vanglia, otherwise Dame Rumour, was played by D. B. Wyndham Lewis, and stood her trial before journalists at the Court of King Baluda (G. K. himself with a tinfoil crown). Among others in the play were Aubrey Hammond, the famous scenic artist, Mrs. Cecil Chesterton and her charming secretary, Bunny Dunham, and Cecil Palmer the publisher.

In one part of the play—which was more like a revue in its presentation—I had to represent the Spirit of the Genteel Press. The Producer told me it was essential that I wore white spats. I had none, of course, having always regarded them as the prerogative of Advertising Men, so I was in a fix. At noon on The Day I fortunately ran into artist Philip Swinnerton, brother of novelist Frank Swinnerton, who said he knew a neighbour

SPECIAL ENGAGEMENT

(by permission of their respective managements) of :

G. K. CHESTERTON	as	King Baluda and Famine.
BUNNY DUNHAM	,,	Freesia of Fulham.
CECIL PALMER	,,	Court Chamberlain and Suburban Twin.
KEITH CHESTERTON	,,	The Dumb Woman.
D. B. WYNDHAM LEWIS	,,	Vanglia the Witch.
HUGH MARTIN	,,	News Editor, Editor and Night Editor.
AUBREY HAMMOND	,,	Lady Reporter and Suburban Twin.
JIM BARNES NEIL McINTYRE VICTOR BOURNE	,,	Reporters.
C. W. SHEPHERD	,,	The Genteel Press.
LOUIS J. McQUILLAND	,,	The Boost Press.
HERBERT GARLAND	,,	The Press of Purity.
W. R. TITTERTON	,,	A Ghost.
SEWELL STOKES JIM BARNES W. R. TITTERTON VICTOR BOURNE	,,	Newspaper Features.
ADA ROBINS	,,	Stone-hand and News Boy.
ANNE PAGE	,,	Suburban Mother and Queen Victoria.
GEORGE HESELTINE	,,	Suburban Father.
BETTY MARTIN	,,	Suburban Daughter.
GEOFFREY HOWARD	,,	Chronicler.

CROWD: MOLLIE TITTERTON, E. V. ODLE, J. COLBERT, SEAN BUSTEED, etc., etc., etc.

Cast of " ST. VANGLIA : The Witch of Fleet Street," an impromptu satire given by journalists before a hard-bitten Fleet Street audience.

who had some spats, and that he would borrow them and bring them around to the Hall an hour before the performance, when we would be having a so-called rehearsal.

At the appointed time, Swinnerton came round with a brace of spats, explaining that they were rather wet because he had found them to be brown spats, whereas I wanted white spats, and that he had whitewashed them. All I had to do to make them white, he said, was to dry them, the whitewash looking like mud at the moment. This I tried at the stove, with G. K. C. giving me advice on how spats should be dried. In the end they were piebald, but I wore them all the same.

I have mentioned that the dialogue was mainly impromptu, which made it rather ticklish, for you never knew what was going to be fired at you. It was rather like being on the Brains Trust, only quicker. Moreover, there was an undercurrent of trying to catch each other out. The genial Cecil Palmer was rather good at this, but he met his match in The Breakfast Scene.

This scene showed a suburban family at breakfast, each reading a different morning paper : it was a scene which offered plenty of scope for cracks of the Fleet Street kind. There were father and mother at opposite ends of the table, with the children around. Aubrey Hammond, the scenic artist, who was six-foot four and 17 stones in weight, was dressed as a Boy Scout. Cecil Palmer, no lightweight himself, was a schoolboy, with satchel.

The mother was pouring out imaginary coffee when Little Cecil looked up from his paper and asked :

" Mother, what's *lust* ? "

But that priceless girl was equal to the occasion.

" That's all right, sonny," she answered, " just eat up your porridge and grow into a strong man, and you'll know what lust is right enough."

I think this was what is called handling a delicate subject fearlessly.

*　　*　　*　　*

I have another story to tell of Palmer. It concerns that amiable old story-teller, Eden Phillpotts, who, though greatly advanced in years, can still produce a good Devonshire story. He once invited Cecil to spend a week-end with him at his house in Torquay. Accordingly Cecil packed a large attaché case with the week-end's necessities and prepared to go. It so happened that he met a friend who asked him where he was going, and Cecil, quite proudly I expect, said that he was going to spend the week-end with Eden Philpotts.

" H'm, where's your luggage ? " asked the friend

Cecil pointed to his case

" You'll want more than that," said the other, who was not unacquainted with the famous novelist's style of living.

But Cecil did not take the hint ; he just said : " This holds all I want," and a few minutes later was on his way to Paddington.

Some hours later, as his train was drawing into Torquay station, he saw Eden Phillpotts waiting on the platform to greet him. Immediately the train stopped, Cecil grasped his case and leapt out. Suddenly the case sprang open and scattered his belongings, from tooth-brush to pyjamas, on the platform. Now if anything makes a man look foolish, it is a contretemps of this kind, and it was with as much confusion as haste that Cecil scrambled his things together, wondering what sort of a clumsy fellow Phillpotts thought he was.

When he at last looked up, there was no sign of the author. He had vanished.

Mystified, Palmer made his way to the station exit and, just as he reached it, Phillpotts came running up the last few yards of the station approach, out of breath.

" My dear Palmer," he begged, " forgive me for not being here to meet you."

Was ever such courtesy shown by host to guest ? Never ; yet there was more to come.

Either Phillpotts did not notice the size of Cecil's case, or he assumed that he had sent a larger one to the house by an outside porter. However, no mention of luggage was made, and not until the dressing-bell went for dinner did Cecil begin to learn the dread facts of the situation. He was expected to come down in glad-rags ; and, to make matters worse, he had already met other guests who, at that very moment, were no doubt donning their dress clothes.

On his way downstairs he caught a fleeting glimpse of Phillpotts who, apparently, did not see him. Then he joined the others, having decided that to apologise would be worse than saying nothing. Then It Happened Again. In came Phillpotts in the same old plus-fours which he had been wearing at the station !

Was there ever such etc., etc., etc. ? Never.

After that Cecil enjoyed the evening, particularly a final chat with the novelist *à deux* over a glass of whisky.

" You'll find your room all right ? " were the last words of Phillpotts, as he accompanied his guest to the foot of the stairs. Cecil said he would.

But he didn't. He wandered into the room of a middle-aged lady, but left just in time to stop her raising an alarm.

The last picture of this series is of Cecil sitting on his bed, wishing he had a Bradshaw to tell him the time of the next train back to Town.

Be it said, however, that on the next day his luck changed. Nothing untoward happened and he spent a happy week-end.

But was there ever so much etc., etc. ? Never.

CHAPTER IX.

COUNTRY CHAPTER : RUS IN URBE

WITHIN that bond which links all newspapermen, you will find lesser bonds, such as those of county, culture, similarity of interests, which are none the less strong because they are imperceptible. I count among my friends quite a number of countrymen by birth or adoption, and frequent meetings with men like J. Wentworth Day and Pat Murphy, who bring the smell of a newly-turned furrow into a newspaper, keep alive one's love of the countryside.

Therefore I dedicate this chapter to " those blue remembered hills, those spires, those farms,"—to misquote Housman. As I mentioned earlier, I am " A Shropshire Lad," and my memory of that lovely county—often renewed—has never ceased to be my inward companion in this, London's most sophisticated street. I have written about the countryside from every angle—stories, articles, poems—and I have broadcast upon it.

Perhaps the most popular nature writer in any London newspaper is Frances Pitt, whose weekly articles in the *Evening News* are avidly read, even by those to whom the ash is as the oak, or the curlew as the snipe. This is not prompted by the fact that she is a Shropshire woman, but by a deep-felt admiration for articles which have created in thousands of townsfolk an interest, even a love, of the furred and feathered folk of the countryside. It is remarkable that the average Londoner can scarely distinguish half-a-dozen garden birds. But he reads his Frances Pitt, all the same.

We must admit that she is lucky in her garden, for, taking her articles over a period, it would seem to have been visited by an amazing variety of birds. Knowing her old house in the Severn Valley, I can well credit it, though this did not deter me once making a crack on the subject at the expense of Jimmy Day, and perhaps at Miss Pitt's, too.

James Wentworth Day, whom I have limned in the chapter " Fleet Street Chaps," was one of our greatest authorities on the countryside and the sports it provides. I met him one day on

his return from a shoot when he had secured a " bag " which
he said, would make any sportsman's mouth water. It included
he told me, triumph tripping up his words, three snipe, two
widgeon, six mallard, three woodcock, a hare and a wild goose.

" Bless my soul, Jimmy," I exclaimed. " Where were you
shooting ? In Frances Pitt's back garden ? "

As readers of the *Daily Mail* know, Pat Murphy can bring
a farm to life in the printed page. Good-looking in "that Irish
way," and standing a full six-foot-three, Pat is not a man to be
overlooked in any company. He is a farmer with the happy
knack of presenting hard facts wrapped up in romance. It is
difficult to read even the most factual of Pat's articles without
sniffing the country air behind them.

He is an incurable romanticist. I once met him when he had
journeyed from the country by train, and learnt that he had spent
the time writing a charming country poem of which I quote
three verses :—

> " I saw a gold-eyed hawk
> Alight upon a pine,
>   And scan the grass beneath
> For wherewithal to dine.
>
> Shrewd sparrows sought the bushes,
> Each mouse its tiny hole,
>   A blackbird clucked alarm
> And warned a lowly mole.
>
> A chaffinch called a robin,
> A robin told a wren,
>   That here was more to fear
> Than the cruelty of men."

In case you think this fantasy, let me say that birds have an
almost telegraphic system of warning when a hawk appears in the
vicinity. Not infrequently this warning becomes a rallying-call
for a host of little birds to make a dead set at this autocrat of
the skies, and drive him in confusion from the district.

Next time I met Pat he was busy on a book—about rabbits—
written from the sociological angle, it being a Murphy contention

hat there is a similarity between the social order of the warren
nd that of humans. He was in some difficulty about a title for
he book, and had been discussing the matter with Bruce Blunt,
ountryman also, and entertaining cookery expert of the *Daily
Express.* Having regard to rabbits' breeding propensities, Bruce
uggested that a good title would be " Colney Hatch." I went a
ittle further regarding the progenitiveness of coneys, and
uggested " Warren Hastings." After that, Murphy thought it
etter to work out a title on his own.

The tall, strong-featured Simon Evans, Postman-Poet of
hropshire, was a friend of mine. Simon became a postman
ecause lung trouble, contracted in the last war, demanded an
pen-air existence. Thus he came to Cleobury Mortimer, by
he Clee Hills in Shropshire, and soon became a familiar figure
n that delectable countryside. His rounds took him in all
veathers across hill and valley, by farm and stream—often a good
ighteen miles a day—and soon Simon wanted to find expression
or the beauties he saw and the simple people he met. First he
urned to poetry, then to books. " Round About the Crooked
teeple " was one : " Shropshire Days and Shropshire Ways "
nother. As a broadcaster from Midland Regional he also became
ell-known.

Poor old Simon ! In the former book he made frequent
uotations from a poem I wrote about the pub at Hopton Wafers,
little village near Cleobury Mortimer, without mentioning the
ame of the author. He was positively mortified when I met him
or the first time and joked about it. He did not know who had
ritten it, he said, but had heard snatches of it here and there,
s it had become an accepted local rhyme. Even the children
t Hopton Wafers school had been taught it by their schoolmaster.
Here are extracts from it :—

> " I'd have you know John Whitehead's ' Crown '
> Where the road runs up and the brook runs down,
> His creaking sign, and 'sturtiums red,
> And windows diamond-laced with lead.
> At Hopton Wafers stands the ' Crown,'
> Where the road runs up and the brook runs down."

(I should mention that the inn stands at the foot of a steep
hill, with a brook singing along beside it.)

It continued :—

> " I'd have you note his rafters black,
> With hams and onions on the rack,
> And the ancient screen, where old men sit,
> And drink their drop and talk their bit,
> As they do each night at Whitehead's ' Crown '
> Where the road runs up and the brook runs down.
>
> I'd have you note his cider's hue,
> In shining cups of white and blue,
> Like evening sun-glow on the sea
> When crested blue holds mastery.
> You'd like the cider at the ' Crown,'
> Where the road runs up and the brook runs down.
>
> But most of all I'd have you rest
> At the ' Crown ' by night when I like it best,
> When the lamps are lit, and shadows grow,
> And old John talks of long ago,
> For then I know you'd love the ' Crown '
> Where the road runs up and the brook runs down."

To those who ask—is there any money in poetry ? I would
say that the full version of the above verses were for some years
a constant source of small revenue. They were reprinted in a
variety of publications, also as a song and as the basis of a
one-act play.

On the publication of his next book, Simon Evans did a gracious
and typical thing. He asked me to let him have another poem
of mine, " The Crooked Steeple," to use as an introduction, and
he mentioned me generously in his foreword.

Simon's lung trouble overcame him in the end, and his
vigorous, striding figure was no more hailed each morning by
the countryfolk whom he served. He and I had become great
friends, and, whenever I could go to " those parts," we would
often sit yarning long into the night. He was particularly fond of
Gray's Elegy, and it seems fitting to quote from it :—

" One morn we missed him on the customed hill,
Along the heath and near his favourite tree ;
Another came ; nor yet beside the rill,
Nor up the lawn nor at the wood was he."

* * *

Shortly before the Coronation, Larry Morrow, a B.B.C. producer, asked me, as a writer on country topics, if I would go to some remote place, spend Coronation Day there, and record my impressions for London National.

The choice of the village was left to me, so I promptly named a little place in Shropshire—none other than Cleobury Mortimer, where Simon Evans was living. It was arranged that I should go there on the day before the Coronation, which took place on the Wednesday. Tuesday afternoon, therefore, saw me leave the B.B.C. armed with a railway pass and the prospect of a comfortable fee afterwards.

It was one of the foulest days of the year, raining torrentially from morn till night. It augured ill for the Coronation. As I sat in the train, with the rain lashing the windows, I began to feel a little less confident of the matter in hand. I had never broadcast before, and the spectre of having nothing worth while to say began to loom before me. There would, I imagined, be bell-ringing, tea for the schoolchildren and so on. There would probably be more rain as well. That would be about all.

I put up at a cosy inn, and later Simon Evans came round to see me. We spent a lively night with some of the locals, and I went to bed feeling that I might not make such a bad job of it after all.

Next day proved the antithesis of its predecessor and I walked into the sunny street to see the locals busy refixing the flags and bedraggled bunting with which the rain had made considerable sport. Not a shop or house was there which had not put up a brave show of decorations. Then I was given a programme of the day's events, which included judging the prizewinners for the best decorated houses and shops. There were several classes in the competition, one of them being for houses with a rateable value of *less than* £6 ! Here was a point to talk about, anyhow.

Then I learned that in the afternoon there was to be a fancy dress procession around the village. Things were looking up.

At eleven o'clock, the bells rang out from the old crooked steeple, and here again I was in luck. The church has a large Norman porch, the walls of which are adorned with carved stone heads, most of which had their noses knocked off when Cromwell's men stabled their horses in the church. A few locals were standing in the porch, and one of them, looking at the noseless faces, observed :—

"Old Crommle hadn't got no use for kings, mister. It'd make him think a bit if he could see us here to-day putting another on 'em on the throne."

How little did the old man think that those words of his would, in a few days' time, be heard by millions of people.

An hour later, there began to arrive in the village a trickle of chaps from the outlying districts, already grotesquely dressed for the afternoon's procession. There were niggers, clowns, an ancient Roman, an old fellow in a century-old linen smock, and many other types besides. They had come early to view the decorations and to drink the King's health as many times as they could, bearing in mind that processions make a call upon the vertical.

Eventually came the procession, with the whole countryside there to see it. It was led by a scratch band playing one lusty march after another. The most amusing participant in the procession was, however, a red, white and blue dog, trotting along as though he well realised the importance of the occasion. I soon learned the story of the dog. He was white by nature, but on the preceding night had found himself mixed up in some rain-soaked bunting which had dyed him in patriotic colours. Then, his master being in the procession, he must, of course, join in.

For the rest of the day there was free beer for one and all at the school and, needless to say, a dance in the evening.

My " talk " could hardly fail now. Nor did it. I recorded it at the B.B.C. on the Friday and listened to myself on the Saturday in a feature called " Coronation Carnival." The procession was the star piece. How grateful I was to those who took part in it—the " men from the barn and the forge and the mill and the fold."

*   *   *

For a time I lived in a village some twenty miles out of London, and there I met an extraordinary character called Old Japhet, about whom I wrote an article for the local paper. There was an amusing sequel.

One day Old Japhet was found lying dead beside a footpath. A passer-by took him to be resting in the heat of the day. Then he discovered that Japhet would not wake again. An opened box of matches was in his hand, and his pipe lay very near. He had died when he was happy, a poppy-flecked field of wheat before his eyes.

Japhet—he was known in no other way, for none knew his surname—was a worker in the fields. He would trim a hedge and be proud of it, and that was as much as Japhet wanted. He lived alone in a hut, and would speak to you of the happiness of lonely men. His age was almost as indefinite as his surname, for his wrinkled face—lean, brown and shaved to the bone—defied speculation.

His dress was peculiar, for he was a peculiar man. In winter he would come down from his hut so muffled in overcoats that you would hardly believe so sturdy a bulk contained so small a man. In summer he was equally picturesque. Slight and lithe—dark trousers, blue-black flannel shirt, a well-worn leather waistcoat, and a belt fastened by some mysteriously embossed clasp—that was Japhet.

Japhet knew beasts, birds and frogs as friends, and herbs were an open book to him. He could tell you where the mandrake grows, and few know that. In spring he could show you the nests of twenty different kinds of birds. Of wrens, he once said to me :—

" Why, their eggs aren't as big as peas, and no wonder, for the bird herself's no bigger nor a bumbly-bee."

From which you will see that Japhet did not go far from nature for his similes. He had an alluring way of adding " y " to his words. He would come down from his hut and tell you how his hat had been lifted high into the air by a " whirlywind." He did not suffer gladly the foolish or the curious. Sometimes he would leave the village for a spell and return, surprised that anyone should ask where he had been. His keen eyes, blue-grey as a jackdaw's, would fix you as he replied : " Leave my business alone. I've been away and I've come back. That's enough."

But he was a kindly man, for who but a kindly man would carry in his pockets tit-bits for the village dogs ?

I had rung up the editor of the local paper, published in a little town some distance away, asking if he would like an article on the passing of Japhet, and he said he would. So I wrote the article, rather on the lines of what I have written above, and sent it to him. I rang him up the following day to see what he thought of it.

" A very fine article, Mr. Shepherd," he said. " Why, it's almost a *photograph* of the old man   In fact, I'm going to pay you for it at photograph rates. I've marked you down for seven-and-sixpence."

There was a further sequel which led to my doing a job which I imagine has fallen to few newspapermen. The vicar called on me to say how much he had enjoyed the article.

" Admirable," he said. " I didn't know the old man myself, but, judging by your article, he must have been a very interesting old fellow."

How odd it is that the clergy can sometimes be so detached ! Everyone in the village knew old Japhet, including myself, a mere sojourner. But the vicar ? No. Yet Japhet was as God-fearing a man as you would wish to meet. I frequently strolled through the woods on Sunday evenings to his hut, and always I found him dressed in an ancient black suit—his " Sunday best."

The vicar then told me he was about to take his annual holiday, and suggested that I might edit the parish magazine which would be going to press in his absence. This was a new one on me. It meant that I would have to write a page of my own instead of the usual parochial matter. Despite his detachment, he was a good scout, so I promised to do as he asked, though I felt rather like a child being entrusted with firearms. There was no knowing what might happen.

However, I kept within the bounds of propriety, though I certainly " struck a new note in parochial journalism " and produced an entertaining page. There was a lively note about quaint parish registers, a nature piece about the gamekeeper's " larder," a parish " quiz," a poem of my own about a country funeral and a little homily on the need for real thankfulness at harvest festivals. On his return the vicar was most complimentary, so I had to assume that I had been a success.

My pen has frequently landed me into trouble, but never into such a packet as it did when I wrote an article for a London newspaper entitled :

WHERE NOBODY WORKS
A Village of Easy Lives and
Cheerful Prosperity

This article nearly made me an outlaw in my own Cleobury Mortimer, my adopted Shropshire village. Someone saw it and sent it anonymously to the nearest local paper, which printed it, asking the question : " Is it Cleobury Mortimer ? " and adding a few comments on its appropriateness. That did it. The next issue of the paper came out with a violent anonymous letter denouncing the article. A copy of it was sent to me in London, and I could see that I must do something about it if I were ever to show my face in the place again. So I wrote a letter to the paper pointing out that I had not even mentioned Cleobury Mortimer, so what ?

This merely served to produce another abusive letter, teeming with personalities. The trouble was that it was partly true of the place in those days. I said : " Nobody works ; at least not in the real sense of the word. The vicar seems to visit nobody ; the barber to shave nobody ; the policeman to arrest nobody ; and the shopkeepers to serve nobody. Everyone has plenty of time, and plenty of tales to tell . . . There are a few shops, but, assuming there to be no subterranean passages, it is a mystery how people do their shopping without being seen. How do the people manage to live with so little effort ? How do they find time to enjoy themselves when people elsewhere are working themselves to skin and grief ? "

All quite true. I managed to clear myself in the end, giving

my anonymous correspondents a good trouncing in the process.
Perhaps the local paper saw the right angle to it in a leaderette
which they published : " The rather racy article, taken from a
London daily, and entitled ' Where Nobody Works ' created a
storm of indignation, amusement and sarcastic comment in the
usually peaceful Cleobury. The proud Salopians have buckled
on their armour, as it were, in self defence, some evidence of which
has been given in our Correspondence columns ; others have
enjoyed hearty laughs over the whole business, and some, even
in their serious moments, have frankly admitted that the particular
scribe hit the nail on the head, if only to a limited extent."

In my early days of short-story writing, I must have had the
best collection of rejection-slips in the country—each one a relic
of some particular disappointment. Yet there was one rejection—
in this case a letter—which I think gave me as much pleasure as
did any acceptance. It was from Sir John Squire, then J. C.
Squire, founder and editor of *The London Mercury*, a monthly
journal devoted to literature in its highest sense. It was quite
the most difficult periodical " to get into " in the country.

J. C. Squire had an international reputation as a poet. To
" sit at the feet of Gamaliel "—in this case Squire—was the
apotheosis of delight for half the intelligentsia of London. I
need not say what it meant to appear in *The London Mercury* !
I was at Kendal at the time, and was reading every book or frag-
ment of Squire which I could secure. I naturally had ambitions
to see something of mine in *The London Mercury* and, not without
trepidation, sent in a country poem which I still think the best
thing I have ever written. Would it appear in company with
John Drinkwater, W. B. Yeats, Edmund Blunden and the rest ?
It didn't! This was the poem. It was called " The Furrow
End."

> " The plough stands idle at the furrow end
> Where Mullard left it but six days ago,
> And half a stubble field lies waiting him
> Who never more will either plough or sow.
> The meadowsweet along the bank,
> The honeysuckle in the lane,
> May bloom and scent a thousand times,
> But he shall never come again.

The sun which glinted on his harness brass,
As with his plough the autumn land he broke,
To-day comes stealing through his damson trees
To catch the brass on well-planed joiners' oak.
Where lavender and thyme perfume,
And bees go heedless through the phlox,
There, on the cleanly red-brick path,
Lies Mullard in his tapered box.

And green-black coats and collars strangely white,
Drawn from the ancient dresser and the chest,
Move in that apple-scented garden there,
Which of all earth old Mullard loved the best.
And now they bear him shoulder-high
To where in quiet lies his wife.
Dead kings with equal words are met :
I am the Resurrection and the Life."

There came back with the poem a note in my hero's own writing. " Dear Mr. Shepherd," it ran. " This misses us by a very narrow margin. Yours sincerely, J. C. Squire."

The verses were published later by Harold Monro, but even its later acceptance was as nothing to Squire's letter.

Meanwhile, I sometimes wonder if they would ever have been written at all, had I not discovered that that early sentence in the Burial Service was a perfect iambic pentameter !

*   *   *

Phillip Holyoake was a descendant of George Jacob Holyoake, founder of the Co-operative movement. But he was more than that ! He was an artist and a countryman. Had he not been the latter, he might have succeeded more as the former, for his love of the countryside induced him to spend many years as the principal of an art school in the Lake District. When he eventually gave this up and came to Fleet Street, he had become old-fashioned, which is no good in these parts. It was a pity, for his robust appearance, his geniality and unfailing humour would soon have made him a perfect " fit-in " in a street where these characteristics are good for a man. But the art school had left its mark upon his work, a fact which unfortunately he could never be made to realise.

When he died some few years ago, a contributing factor to his death was disappointment. Too late he saw that behind all the " go-as-you-please " air of Fleet Street there is a streak as cold as steel, and that it is only a man's work which counts in the end.

Holyoake and I were great friends, and it fell to us to enjoy an artistic adventure as original as it was happy, one which prompted James Dunn (" R. E. Corder "), in the *Newspaper World*, to liken us to the troubadours of old.

Holyoake possessed a lightweight motor-cycle, and we conceived the idea of setting out on it to tour the countryside, making our living as we went, Holyoake doing sketches, and myself writing verses about various rural inns which we encountered. We were to take practically no money with us, except a few shillings in our pockets and a pound sewn in the lining of Holyoake's coat for emergency.

Holyoake weighed sixteen stones and I, the pillion passenger, twelve, so that the little bike was nearly top-heavy. Nevertheless, we started off and made Shrewsbury, after which we said good-bye to towns for a fortnight, and chugged into the rurality of West Shropshire and the Welsh border.

It was too late on the first evening to begin " operations " so we wheeled the bicycle behind a haystack and slept beside it, after a bread-and-cheese supper at a pub. Next day we began our working holiday, and sailed up to a little inn, whereupon Holyoake set up his bamboo easel and began to make a sketch, whilst I went inside and ordered beers for us both, asking the landlord if he had any objection to my friend drawing his pub.

Needless to say, he had none, but came out to watch Holyoake rapidly putting the pub to paper. By this time half the village were standing around watching what, to them, was a miracle being wrought. Meanwhile, I was back in the pub gently hinting to the landlord that a few shillings might buy the picture, and moreover that, if he bought it, I would write some verses to go with it. He promptly agreed, and it was now my job to do the verses. This was not difficult, for the pub was a poem in itself.

Country people are peculiarly susceptible to rhymes, and think the making of them a matter of mysterious skill. Thus, when I had finished mine, and they had been read to the now swelling bar-parlour, the landlord immediately fetched some glue and pasted them on the black oak beam above the fireplace, while a prosperous farmer paid me two shillings for writing out a copy for him to keep at home. As for Holyoake, he positively blushed at the admiration showered on his drawing, and was so touched that he went outside again and with his crayons turned it into a coloured wonder. With the farmer's two shillings we had now made nine-and-six, which was pretty good going with the price of bread-and-cheese and beer what it was then. The verses were simple, but very true :

> " I sing a song of the Bull and Dog
> Which stands on the Shrewsbury road,
> A house of call for the limousine
> Or the carrier with his load.
> Its ancient porch with snug side seats
> And pillars of well-turned oak,
> Are a joy to lovers of all good things,
> Be they rich or humble folk.
>
> But come within to the old fire side
> To sit on the oaken screen,
> And call for beer from the landlord here,
> And learn what beer can mean ;
> For beer at the Bull and Dog is good,
> As good as the folk who serve it,
> And the man who doesn't know good ale
> When he gets it, doesn't deserve it."

All this took us a little over an hour, and soon, after buying a few drinks for the locals, we were on our way. At an old inn some miles away we repeated the process, doing a rougher sketch and a shorter rhyme in return for a meal of home-cured ham and three eggs each. After this, and an afternoon snooze beneath a honeysuckle-laden hedge, the world seemed none too bad.

In the early evening we earned seven-and-six at another inn, and, later, we fetched up at a mellow pub where we did the now usual sketch and verses in return for a bed. It was here that, after supper, the landlord took us into his kitchen and produced a huge stone jar of damson wine, round which we sat long after all good countrymen should have been in bed.

Our difficulty was not to stay too long in one place—not, at least, until we had built up a little reserve. When we had done this, we would often spend a day and a night in a village, and spend our money where we had earned it.

At one inn the landlord produced a fiddle—which I happen to be able to play—and we sat long into the night singing songs. His own favourite song he sang to some nebulous air invented by himself, but I managed to accompany him, with the result that Holyoake thought it time to go to bed. Nevertheless, it was a rare old country song and began :

> " Seated by the fire-side,
> Smoking my long clay—
> A burning log, a glass of grog,
> To keep dull care away."

It was at this pub that they christened two young ferrets " Poet " and " Painter." I should mention that Holyoake, if he particularly liked an inn, would give them a quick water-colour for their money, as he did in this case.

At the week-end we " struck oil " by discovering a landlord progressive enough to be thinking of having a booklet done about his inn, which was really a small hotel with a quaint farmhouse attached. In return for my writing the booklet and Holyoake doing the illustrations we were given a perfect week-end.

Here again I had to copy out my verses a second time, in this case for a sporting rector, whose customary breath would have seriously disturbed the House of Convocation. He paid us with a dozen apricots, picked warm in the sunny rectory garden. These were the verses :

> " The road it runs from Welshpool
> Along to Shrewsbury town,
> And passes many a pasture
> And many a ploughland brown ;

And many a ploughland brown, my lads,
Till Churley comes in view,
Where the cheer is good and the beer is good
For the likes of me and you,
For the likes of me and you, my lads,
For the likes of me and you.

The Lion gives the cheer I mean
And sells the beer as well,
So come with me into the bar
And let the company swell ;
And let the company swell, my lads,
And sing a song or so,
For this is the place where you make your pace
Be it either fast or slow,
Be it either fast or slow, my lads,
Be it either fast or slow."

So we went on. Despite our regular entertainment of thirsty
natives, we managed to finish the holiday with a pound or two to
the good, after which we did articles, illustrated and otherwise, for
various papers and magazines. Altogether we did very well out
of it, but our greatest profit lay in our memories of kindly countryfolk, lamp-lit rooms, friendly dogs, good ale, old songs, clinking
anvils, fantails on russet roofs and—yes—thick, curling slices of
home-cured ham, sizzling in their own brown liquor, and with
gleaming poached eggs lying on 'em.

TUDOR BUILDINGS IN FLEET STREET, WITH INNER TEMPLE
GATEWAY BELOW
Drawn by EDWARD SWANN

CHAPTER X

FLEET STREET ANIMALS

WITH all respect to my friend Nathaniel Gubbins, I have to say that one cat in this chapter cuts a sorry figure. Not every cat is a Sally the Cat. With further respect to Nat—Dog-Detestor No. 1—I have to admit also to glamorising an odd dog or two. It can't be helped; the dogs just seem to imbibe Fleet Street eccentricity more than the cats do.

Fleet Street cats have a rather poor time of it. They are mainly caretakers' cats, stuck away at the tops of high buildings with a hundred-foot drop to the nearest dust-bin, and nothing but a tray of cinders in which to take their airing. If they are not caretakers' cats, then they are shop cats, and being a shop cat is not much of a job, especially on Sundays. Shop cats are left alone in the shops over the week-end to catch mice, and you can see them on Sundays, sitting forlornly behind plate-glass windows, on empty slabs which are normally meant for buns.

But with Fleet Street dogs it is different. Most of them live in pubs, and, in this respect, I should hate to hear silly comparisons made between them and newspapermen. There is, of course, a sprinkling of cats also in the pubs, but such cats carry an indifferent, almost disapproving air with them, whereas dogs seem to appreciate that they are living in interesting surroundings.

The most famous dog in Fleet Street was Scamp, of the " Cock Tavern." He was there for a number of years but passed on a little time ago, with a valedictory glance at the veterinary surgeon. He was a thick-set, brown-and-white terrier with a low chassis.

Scamp had a passion for pennies. You would be feeling in your pocket for change when a paw would lightly tap your foot, and you would look down to see Scamp asking for a penny. You tossed one to him which he would catch adroitly ; then he would trot away with the penny in his mouth. A few minutes later he would be doing the same thing to someone else ; this would go on until he had six pennies in his mouth. Then, as though a hornet had stung him, he would tear out of the pub and take the pennies to a man who had a newspaper pitch a few yards away.

Nobody ever knew how many sixpences the man collected in this way, but as Scamp worked pretty assiduously during opening hours, it must have been a good number. There were two inexplicable angles to this. You could try your best to make Scamp open his mouth when he had, say, four pennies in it, but you might as well have tried to lift Olympus. Scamp's jaws were clamped. Yet as soon as he had caught two more pennies, away he would streak to the newspaper seller. He never went with less than six ; nor did anyone ever see him catch a seventh. Either he could count, or six were all he could hold without spilling them. The other unexplainable part was how the partnership between him and the man began. It was not a matter of food, for the man never gave him anything for his money. The newspaper seller was asked many times to explain, but he never gave away the secret.

Eventually customers were asked by the " Cock Tavern " to refuse Scamp's requests for coins—not that he was a nuisance, for he was too gentle for that—but because he developed a gangrenous mouth due to copper poisoning.

Most dogs, if you aim a soda-syphon at them, will be out of range before you can say " knife." Not so with Scamp. He *liked* soda-water and would open his mouth so that you could squirt it in. I have seen him take nearly half a syphon of it, the jet disappearing down his throat like a crystal ribbon.

Scamp's sagacity never showed itself more than when he wished to cross the street from the pavement outside the " Cock." Being a narrow street, Fleet Street's traffic was highly congested, and Scamp had had some narrow squeaks in trying to cross it ; indeed, on one occasion he had gone under the front of a bus, and come out at the back of it.

Friends of Scamp, seeing him standing mournfully on the edge of the kerb, would often lead him across to the opposite side. Eventually Scamp grew into the habit of accosting any passer-by of whom he had a mental or olfactory record, barking to be led across. So well known was he that he rarely failed to find an escort.

Famous as he was, however, he might have been more so, had it not been for his own obstinacy. It was fixed that " Fleet Street's Famous Dog " was to be put on the air by the B.B.C.

in " In Town To-night." A commentator was to speak about him, after which the Famous Dog was to bark. Unfortunately, the Famous Dog refused to bark, good as he was at it, and the project was a fiasco.

Not far from the " Cock Tavern " is the " Clachan," a small but historic tavern which is mentioned, with others, in my chapter on taverns. Here lived a most authoritative dog, a dog of purpose. Whenever closing time came, he would begin to take an interest in affairs, watching carefully the exit of journalists and others. Invariably there would be a little group of men endeavouring to conclude an argument at the last minute. That is where Rex would come in. He would sneak round and nip first one ankle, then another, of the lingerers, ushering them out as you may have seen a sheep-dog round sheep into a pen. The fact was that Rex actually was a sheep-dog, and had had an early training on the Welsh hills.

There once walked Fleet Street a journalist named Hilgrave— that was not his name, but it will suffice—on whom the sun shone but occasionally, and then only wanly. Adversity, as he said, was his second name. His chief trouble was that his real love was poetry, and, as everyone knows, there is little to be made out of verse. To support himself in his application to the Muse, he did free-lance journalism, and, as he was too dreamy to bother about facts, prose was almost as unremunerative to him as poetry. But he was a scholar, a good talker, a good listener and a good chap. Moreover, he never borrowed. All this made him popular in Fleet Street, and it was many years before he could tear himself away and go abroad, as eventually he did.

Now being hard-up throughout the year is one thing, but being broke at Christmas is another. It was therefore unfortunate that one Christmas found Hilgrave absolutely " on the floor." He was living alone in a small attic in Gunpowder Alley, one of those many intersecting courts which lay behind the north side of Fleet Street before they were blitzed out of existence.

Hilgrave had managed to scratch up some sort of a Christmas dinner, but it was not enough to prevent him being hungry in the evening. Consequently he went round to a small pub and asked them to cut him a couple of sandwiches. He would have asked for more than a couple, but his pocket forbade. These he deposited in his attic; then, as a sop to melancholy, he took a stroll into the night. He sighed as he looked at Anderton's Hotel in Fleet Street, and thought of the warmth and food within.

His walk took him through several interesting courts such as Pemberton Row, Wine Office Court and Red Lion Court, and it was in the latter that he encountered a dog who looked as solitary as himself. Hilgrave patted the dog, who in turn licked his hand. As he continued his walk, the dog followed and it seemed to Hilgrave that he had met one in similar straits to his own.

When he arrived at his own door, the dog was still with him, and looked pleadingly as Hilgrave opened the door. It seemed cruel to turn the dog away, for it was snowing slightly and very cold. Hilgrave thought it over. He had only two sandwiches, but—well—hang it all, the dog should have one of them. After all, it was Christmas night. So up the rickety stairs they went.

As Hilgrave pictured it to me, it must have been a touching sight—almost Dickensian. When the meal was finished, something prompted Hilgrave to turn back the thick fur on the dog's neck and see what name was on the collar. If any man ever felt he had been made a fool of, it was Hilgrave when he caught sight of two words : ANDERTON'S HOTEL.

" So that's where you come from, you little devil," he said. " Living all day on turkey and roast beef, eh ? And then you come round here and eat half my sandwiches. You can just get to hell out of it."

So saying, he took the dog downstairs and pushed him into the bleakness of Gunpowder Alley.

To-day only a great gap on the north side of Fleet Street tells where the old-fashioned residential Anderton's Hotel once stood. Many imagine that gap to be the result of a bomb, but actually the hotel was pulled down just before the war to make room for a more modern building.

It had a certain popularity with newspapermen, for there was always a night porter on duty, and you could get a bed at any hour. Often when I was working with the *Daily Mail* I would leave the office at perhaps midnight, and, after a drink at the Press Club, make a bee line for Anderton's. The trouble was, however, that you might bump into a bunch of other newspapermen in the lounge and make a night of it.

* * *

Never was there a more famous bird than the " old " parrot at the " Cheshire Cheese," so called to distinguish him from the bird which took his place when he died a few years ago, and when over 200 newspapers throughout the world gave him obituary notices. He was the most original thing that ever grew feathers. Even his arrival at the " Cheese " was marked by originality. Mr. Moore, whose family owned the old tavern, was in the habit occasionally of giving a box of cigars to a grizzled sea-captain on shore leave when he came to Fleet Street. On one occasion, the old man arrived at the " Cheese " with a square parcel for Mr. Moore, who was not in the tavern at the time. The captain just gave the parcel, which was the size of a box of 100 cigars, to a barmaid, asking her to give it to Mr. Moore on his return. Then she put it on a shelf and thought no more about it until later in the day, when her colleague behind the bar suddenly said :

" There's something *alive* in that box! "

Mr. Moore happened to come in at that moment, and hastily opened the parcel, and there in a cigar-box was the parrot on the point of expiring. He was revived and lived to reign in the " Cheese " for forty years. His vocabulary was rich even on his arrival, but he increased it enormously during the years which followed. He learnt to imitate the popping of corks and the gurgle of wine being poured out. He would say " Scotch " when asked what he would like to drink, and he learnt certain words which would make a bargee envious.

One of these words was, in the last war, reserved for the Kaiser. One merely had to say : " What do you think of the Kaiser, Polly?" to get a terse and extremely obscene " —— him! " Just how he had learnt this conversational quip nobody seemed to know, but there were several waggish waiters at the " Cheese " in those days, which may have had some bearing on the matter. The odd thing was that the old bird seemed to have an idea that the word was meant only to be said in anger, and I once witnessed a little drama in which the word came out as appropriately as it might have done in Billingsgate.

It was the custom at quiet times to let Polly out of his cage to roam about the bar and elsewhere. On one occasion someone had given him a well-buttered stick of asparagus which he held in his beak, wondering how he should deal with it. At that moment the " Cheshire Cheese " cat came into the room and, being partial to buttered asparagus himself, seized one end of the stick. There ensued a tug-o'-war which the cat, by superior weight, easily won. Old Polly watched the disappearing asparagus. Then out came the awful word :

" —— him! " he screeched and hopped away disgustedly to his cage.

H.R.H. the Princess Royal once visited the " Cheshire Cheese " in company with the Lord Mayor. She had heard of the famous parrot, of course, and insisted on being introduced to him. The manager did his best to side-track her, but she would not be put off. Fortunately nothing untoward happened. Nobody mentioned the Kaiser!

Polly entertained a host of other high-placed people—Princes, Peers, Ambassadors and visitors from all over the world, and he was present at the famous lunch when Joseph Chamberlain, Mr. Asquith, Sir Edward Grey and Mr. Haldane all ate together at " Ye Olde Cheshire Cheese." The signatures of these notables in the visitors' book are reproduced on page 127.

Polly was once the instrument of one of the best practical jokes played by Fleet Street journalists, which is saying something. A bunch of them were broke one night and endeavoured to persuade the " Cheese " to put their drinks on the " slate," which the manager refused to do.

Now something had to be done about this, and a whispered conference was held, which resulted in one of the party going to the shadowy part of the bar, where the parrot was sitting, and quietly putting the bird inside his overcoat and walking out with him, followed by the others. It had been decided to pawn him.

They went to a pawn-shop in the neighbourhood of Drury Lane, where one of them persuaded " Uncle " to advance them a pound on the parrot, after which they returned to the " Cheese " and ordered a round of drinks. They found a great commotion going on within. The famous parrot, the " Cheese's " greatest asset, was missing!

The manager had an idea as to who was responsible, but this in no way lessened his alarm as to the bird's whereabouts. Presently one of the party said naïvely :

" I *think* I might be able to find him for you."

" Then, for Heaven's sake, do," said the manager. " I'll give anything to have him back. See, I'll give you five pounds if you can do it."

" Very well," said the other, and left the house, as though to look for the parrot. Presently he returned and whispered :

" I've got your parrot."

The manager registered great relief. " Thank God," he said. " Give him to me—quick."

" Let's have the five pounds first," insisted the other, and the money changed hands.

" And now here's your parrot," said our friend as he pressed the pawn-ticket into the manager's hand and disappeared. Of course, the manager had to redeem the parrot at his own expense, but, so glad was he to have the bird back, that he decided to make no fuss about it, and eventually all was forgiven, though never forgotten. That is the story as I have heard it.

Such was the old bird's fame that, when he died, the B.B.C. broadcast the news with almost as much verbal melancholy as they might have applied to a defunct statesman. It was a world broadcast, and newspapers all over the globe picked up the story.

The *New York American* came out with a flash of headlines :

> " FAMED POLLY
> WICKED BIRD
> PASSES OUT
> Notorious Cheshire Cheese in
> Mourning as 40-years-old Expert
> in Profanity dies."

The parrot, of course, was much older, forty years applying merely to his reign at the " Cheese." Even from as far afield as China came obituaries, and the *North China Star* said :

" FAMOUS PARROT OF CHESHIRE CHEESE IS PNEUMONIA VICTIM

Polly was probably the best known parrot in the world . . . She had kissed Princess Mary, ordered ' Scotch ' for Premier Baldwin, answered Philip Snowden's query about the Kaiser with ' —— him! ' He could imitate the popping of a cork and the gurgle of wine being poured."

The *Baltimore Sun* made a feature of Polly's death under the headlines :

" POLLY OF CHESHIRE CHEESE FAME IN LONDON IS DEAD

Parrot that cried ' Scotch ' at Ancient Fleet Street Hostelry to be Stuffed."

Which was true, for the bird was stuffed and is still to be seen on a wall in the annexe of " Ye Olde Cheshire Cheese."

Perhaps the greatest tribute paid to him by Fleet Street came from the *Saturday Review*, which ran a competition for the best epitaph in verse about the departed parrot. The competition was set and judged by James Bone, London Editor of the *Manchester Guardian*, who selected the following as the winner :

" The pop of corks, the gurgle of wine,
Kissing and human speech were mine,
Accomplishments which could not save
Me from a dry and silent grave.

Enough ! No maudlin tear be shed :
Not all of Polly shall be dead.
Though silent, here upon the shelf
I stand—in memory of myself."

G. Rostrenor Hamilton.

The present parrot, although in no way comparable with the old bird, is nevertheless a character and a good mimic. Perhaps when it has been at the hostelry forty-odd years, it will have more to say for itself.

It will have been noticed that in referring to the original Polly I have attributed masculinity to the old rascal. In so doing I have followed what was a fixed Fleet Street custom until the first Armistice Day, November 11th, 1918.

On that day, for the first and last time, Polly laid an egg !

* * *

Another celebrity in Fleet Street is " Goggles," the lop-eared loose-skinned dog of the " Kings and Keys." " Goggles " is a mixture of bull-terrier and goodness-knows-what. He is a big white dog with a black patch surrounding each eye—like a Panda reversed—and the accompanying caricature—which is by Glossop, the well-known artist—has caught him in one of his clown-like moods. " Goggles " is nothing if not a clown, and a series of vastly amusing photographs of him hang in the " Kings and Keys." He is, in fact, the pub's pin-up dog.

Traffic regulations are nothing to him. He will calmly take his bone to the middle of the pavement and there lie and gnaw it, oblivious of the throng stepping over and around him. Sometimes he even tries the same nonchalance in the Street itself, as though he relishes the mighty buses swerving to avoid him.

He has no tricks ; he is just funny. He is also a model father, as fathers go in the dog-world. He once became the parent of a litter of pups by a lady dog attached to a balloon site some distance from Fleet Street. Each day he paid them a morning visit, gave them a lick and lolloped back home.

No accomplishments, but known and loved by the whole of Fleet Street.

* * *

We now come to The Cat Who Cut a Sorry Figure. He lived at " The Two Brewers," which is in Shoe Lane, between the *Daily Express* and the *Evening Standard*. The episode is somewhat dated, for it occurred in the days before the placing of cellophane over counter-snacks came into use.

Tom Cottrell, the black-and-white humorous artist, his brother Reg and I frequently went to the " Two Brewers " for a sandwich lunch at the counter, and, though it was clever of the cat to pick his way among the plates of sandwiches, the feat hardly appealed to those of us who were going to eat them.

GOGGLES: THE FLEET STREET PHILOSOPHER
("It depends on what you mean by *Bone*")
Caricature by Glossop

Pushing the cat off the counter was a failure, for the animal would be back again as soon as your head was turned. Eventually, Reg Cottrell took the matter in hand one evening, when we were the only three in the bar. There was the cat, as usual, stepping nimbly towards the sandwiches. Reg " puss-pussed " him into reach ; then he said to his brother Tom :

" Now, Tom, you just stroke him very slowly from head to rump, and, when your hand touches his tail, let go."

Tom did this, forgetting that the process usually ends in the cat's tail going bolt upright, as it did on this occasion. Meanwhile Reg, standing behind him, had picked up a soda-water syphon, ice-cold from the cellar.

The rear view which the cat presented offered a perfect target, and Reg let loose with the syphon—Fiz-z-z !

The cat gave a wild screech and, with a flying leap, went clean through a leaded glass partition and disappeared from view. We had to pay for the mending of the glass, of course, but it was worth it, for the cat was never seen again among the sandwiches.

I have asked Tom to draw his impressions of the incident and his drawing is reproduced here.

TOM COTTRELL depicts himself (left) and his brother Reg in the episode : " The Cat Who Cut a Sorry Figure "

CHAPTER XI

The Tavern's Open Door

It is to be expected that Fleet Street, being concerned almost entirely with journalism and its offshoots, should have its own particular kind of pubs. In this way the Street does not disappoint, for its many taverns, most of them with centuries-old histories, are as individual as the men who have used, and still use them—from Dryden to Dr. Johnson ; from Johnson to Dickens and Thackeray ; from these illustrious two to G. K. Chesterton, and from him to the moderns of to-day, whose wit, as I have already maintained, is every bit as good as that of their predecessors.

Newspapermen are generally assumed to be a race fond of its liquor. This has been said persistently by the admiring and malicious alike. I would rather have it that journalists are men who always have something worth saying and something worth laughing at, and that they instinctively congregate where they are sure of meeting others who also possess those priceless qualities. If you can tell me of any more likely place than a pub for this happy conjunction to occur—well, I shall be much obliged.

The average newspaperman is less inclined to say " I am going out for a drink " than to say " I'm going up to the ' Cheese ' " or " I think I'll look in at the ' Falstaff.' " You see what I mean ?

The pubs of Fleet Street are, to the working writers and artists —I am excluding the high-ups, of course—a definite part of their background, and as such are looked upon with affection. As an example of this I quote some verses sent to me from Africa by a journalist-soldier—six-foot-three, amiable John Abraham.

> " The stately pubs of Fleet Street,
> How beautiful they stand !
> This desert waste reminds me of
> Their spittoons full of sand.

Their barmaids blonde and beautiful
We saw but to the waist,
Behind their pump-lined battlements,
So lady-like, so chaste !

I loathe the scents of Egypt,
The frankincense and myrrh ;
I'd swap the lot for one pint pot
Of Charrington or Meux.

The Cock, the Bell, the Cogers,
The Albion and the Lud ;
If any bomb fell on them,
I pray that it were dud.

The portraits in the Falstaff
Do not include my own,
But from those Fleet Street taverns
I, with the great, was thrown.

Poppin's has seen great argument
About it and about ;
And evermore a bigger bore
Came in when one went out.

The crowded pubs of Fleet Street,
The Mitre, Cheshire Cheese ;
A hundred NAAFI canteens
I'd trade for one of these.

The Ad-man's double whisky,
The virgin's gin-and-lime.
I'll buy again in Fleet Street
When Hitler calls it ' Time ' ! "

John Abraham's verse by no means exhausts the stately—
which none of them is—pubs of Fleet Street. Only a few steps
down the various little courts mentioned in another chapter, one
comes across taverns so tucked away that none but habituees of
the Street would find them—the Red Lion, Welsh Harp, Rose
and Crown, and the rest.

Indeed, the Welsh Harp is actually unknown to many news-papermen, particularly those of the new generation in the Street. It hides in a little-frequented court called Lombard Alley, and on one of its windows, in bold, worn lettering, you see YE OLDE RUM HOUSE ; SHIP'S RUM ONLY.   Truly there must have been a time when even a bad cold had its compensations.

This quiet pub has always done a small trade in lunches and suppers for printers and, quite often, for journalists.   There was once a landlord there, full of ambition, who decided to have a one-item menu card daily on the well-scrubbed tables. One day I saw, to my mystification, a crudely written card announcing the day's dish as

OXTAILS AND HORNICATS

This baffled me as much as it did others, until I discovered that the landlord, in his effort to lift the pub socially had tried to remember "Haricot Oxtail," which he had read in some other place.

The Falstaff is as much a restaurant as a bar, and mid-day sees it crowded with all types of toilers in newspaperdom, from women journalists to advertising men.   To-day the preponderance lies with the latter to the irk of editorial people.   There is always a friendly antipathy between these two sections of the Street, each of which prefers its own company to the other.   Editorial men say it is *they* who make the papers, while the Ad-men declare that but for *them* there would be no jobs for journalists.   It is rather like the old question of which came into the world first— the hen or the egg ?

John Abraham's reference to the " Ad-man's double whisky " is not made lightly, for the advertising men are certainly on the more lucrative side of the game.   I was once in the Falstaff with a colleague who glanced at the clientele, at that moment mainly composed of advertising representatives.

" And to think those chaps are mentioned in the Bible," he said wistfully.   " Yes, there is mention of advertising men in the old Book."

" Where ? " I asked.

" I forget just where," said my friend, " but its in that bit which says ' They grin like dogs and run about the city.' "

The Falstaff makes no claim to antiquity, but it is unique

in that its walls are hung with scores of photographs of well-known newspapermen, most of them " snapped " in the down-stairs bar where they hang. It was here that I once met that great tenor, the late Ben Davies, of whom artist Donaldson tells a good story.

Don is a Fleet Street notability, as much for his talents as his versatility as a raconteur. A dyed-in-the-wool Scot, he is Something in one of the great Scottish clans. Here is his story :

The great man was staying in a small Scottish town which boasted of its glee concerts. What more natural than that Ben Davies should be asked to sing with them at their next concert ? The main glee was to be " Hail, Smiling Morn," in which occur the words rendered in the glee as " Fly-y-ies away ; Fly-y-ies away." It happened at a rehearsal.

Ben was soloist with the rest coming in as an accompaniment. He was at the " Fly-y-ies away " bit when the chorus came in with " Flees awa' ; Flees awa'." Ben looked round to see what had gone wrong, then continued : " Fly-y-ies away ; fly-y-ies away," only to be joined by the chorus again with " Flees awa'." This time Davies stopped and insisted on the matter being sorted out, but neither his fame nor his portly figure could intimidate the rugged Scots tradesman who conducted.

" It's a' richt, Mr. Davies," he said. " Ye may be a great singer, but ye mun remember that ye're in Scotland the noo, and *it's* ' *Flees awa*'." The great man bowed to the decision.

Ye Olde Bell Tavern is at the lower end of Fleet Street, and is entered by an archway which the uninitiated may easily overlook. It is a comfortable little pub with its own clientele, most of whom are newspapermen. It is an institution at the Bell to serve potatoes in their jackets on Saturday nights in winter-time.

There is another entrance from St. Bride's churchyard, and here arises an interesting fact—the Olde Bell was built by Sir Christopher Wren as a hostel for his workmen engaged in building the now famous church. There had been an inn on the site long before this, but the Great Fire destroyed it.

What a man was Christopher ! Not having enough to do in rebuilding half the churches in the City, he must needs design a pub ! This recalls a verse by G. K. Chesterton, illustrated, I believe, by himself. The drawing shows Sir Christopher in the costume of the day, about to leave his " office " in which, with delightful incongruity, a typist sits at her machine. Wrote G.K. :

> " Said Sir Christopher Wren—
> ' I'm going out to dine with some men.
> If anyone calls,
> Say I'm designing St. Paul's.' "

" Poppin's," referred to by John Abraham, is so called because it stands in Poppin's Court. Its real name is the Red Lion, not to be confused with the other Red Lion which stands in Red Lion Court, farther up the Street. The word Poppin's comes from Popyngay Aley, a messuage there bearing the sign of the Poppinjay and belonging to the monks of Cirencester, until the filibustering Henry VIII got hold of it at the dissolution. Poppin's is not the resort of bores which John Abraham's witty verse would suggest. On the contrary, it is a meeting place of some of the cleverest and best-known journalists in Fleet Street.

The Old Cock Tavern must be mentioned here, although it is not actually the same tavern as that which enjoyed a large measure of fame over several centuries. The original Cock stood on the other side of Fleet Street from where stands the present house, and was frequented in its time by Dryden, Dr. Johnson, Dickens and a host of other giants. Nevertheless, when it was pulled down in 1887, when the Bank of England's branch was built, many of its " properties " were transferred to the old building which is the present Cock. You will find there to-day the old oak " pews " which have seen centuries of dinners served in them, likewise the Jacobean mantelpiece ; also the original carved Cock sign, reputed to be the work of Grinling Gibbons.

With these " props " installed, the Cock to-day possesses much of the atmosphere of the old house, and, in normal times, can boast a menu well worthy of the old traditions. Being adjacent to the Temple and the Law Courts, it is frequented mainly by the legal gentry, and the conversation you overhear is more about torts than type.

The accompanying distinguished drawing of the Cock Tavern is by George (" Tommy ") Thompson, the well-known Fleet Street artist.

OLD WINE AND NEW BOTTLES
The Olde Cock Tavern amidst modern surroundings
A Picture by George Thompson

For the true haunt of newspapermen, however, you must go
to Ye Olde Cheshire Cheese—one of the most historic taverns
in the country. It is also one of the most obscure, for it has no
frontage to the Street, the only indication of its presence being
a small, overhanging lamp at the entrance to a dark alley called
Wine Office Court. On the lamp are the words " Ye Olde
Cheshire Cheese." To see the Cheese itself, you have to take
a score of steps up the court, where another lamp indicates an
insignificant doorway, the stone step of which has been so worn
by generations of feet that it is now protected by an iron grid.

Or, instead of going into Wine Office Court, you may turn in
at another little alley a few yards farther on, called Cheshire Court,
which ends in a cul-de-sac at another entrance to the Cheese,
on the walls of which hang photographs of celebrities who have
attended the ceremony of the opening of the " Olde Cheshire
Cheese Pudding " season.

Whichever entrance you choose, you are soon standing where
every floorboard echoes the tread of bygone literary giants. The
Cheese has not changed one whit since it was rebuilt after the
Great Fire. Its oak beams, its panelling, its sawdusted floor are
just the same as when Dr. Johnson lumbered in with his erratic
friend Oliver Goldsmith—the former, no doubt, curling his
tongue round some new definition for his Dictionary, and the
latter working out a chapter for the " Vicar of Wakefield."

Americans adore the Cheese, and, in normal times, visit it by
the hundred each year. No Cheshire Cheese legend—and there
are plenty—is too tall for them, a fact which once prompted one
of Fleet Street's bright spirits to put up some of the floor sawdust
into a bag and sell it to a credulous Yank as being made from
the beams of Nelson's *Victory*. I often wonder if that bag of
sawdust may not even now be reposing in a glass case in some
wealthy New York home.

Take a look round and notice the antiquity of the place ;
hardly a bit of woodwork which is not almost black with age.
There are uneven walls, sloping stairs and undulating floors so
thickly covered with sawdust that it is apt to find its way into
one's shoes and trouser turn-ups. Indeed, this has been known
to find disfavour with journalists returning home late and having

their excuses rejected by observant wives with a knowledge of the Cheese and its sawdust.

The bar looks every year of its three centuries, with its open fire-place, its mellowed walls and small-paned windows. Some might even call it shabby, but what matter so long as it is the comfortable shabbiness of old shoes?

Not only for its antiquity is this little bar dear to newspapermen. It has another claim upon their hearts—most of 'em, anyhow—inasmuch as women are not allowed in it. Not even the incursion of women journalists into Fleet Street has broken down the rule, and the Cheese remains the last stronghold of the men of ink—sanctuary, as was old Alsatia, that haunt of the lawless which lay on the other side of the Street.

There is plenty of room elsewhere in the Cheese for the devotees of gin-and-lime—in the passage or the annexe round the corner, where they may drink under the baleful eye of an earlier parrot in its glass case.

The most notable room in the Cheshire Cheese, however, is the dining-room opposite the bar, for it was used by Dr. Johnson, Goldsmith, Dickens, Thackeray and countless others. Unfortunately, it was severely damaged by a non-enemy fire early in the war, but it is to be restored, as far as possible, to its old self. Here it was that visitors were shown Dr. Johnson's seat at the long oak table, round which sat Oliver Goldsmith and other choice spirits. The other side of the room was furnished with old-fashioned oak pews with hard, cushionless seats, an inconvenience little noticed when the famous Pudding came on.

Probably no dish has ever been so much written or talked about as has the Olde Cheshire Cheese Pudding. I, myself, have seen it served from a great dish capable of satisfying the hunger of eighty people. Its composition was partly a mystery, but it was known to contain rumpsteak, mushrooms, larks, kidneys, oysters and heaven knows what other delicacies.

The serving of it was a ritual, the head waiter dipping into it with all the gravity of a bishop at a font. The Pudding was, in later years, served in the upstairs dining-room—" William's Room "—and the portions sent below at the request of a waiter who would go to the foot of the stairs and bawl " Old Cheshire Cheese Pudding—One ! " (or two—or three—according to the portions needed). This always " fetched " the Americans and other visitors, who thought they were listening to some wonderful echo of the past. But the " echo " blew up with a bang one day.

A friend of mine, Alec Aitkin, and I were standing near the stairs discussing a story when there came the stentorian :

" *Old Cheshire Cheese Pudding—two !* "

Following it immediately came Aitkin's voice, imitative and equally stentorian, with :

" *Newcastle United—one !* "

The place was full at the time, so there is no need for me to describe the volume of the laugh which went round. Even the waiter was overcome and unable to do his turn again. Instead he sent his orders up by the kitchen-boy, fearful that another " Old Cheshire Pudding—Two " would bring him more football results.

Sir Bernard Spilsbury at one time frequently took his meals at the Cheshire Cheese, and it was said by some of the lads, who often took a peep at the famous pathologist through the side window, that he approached his chop in the true dissecting manner.

I have not found his name in the Visitors' Book, but, had I done so, I should have found it in good company. Here are a few names taken at random :

Winston S. Churchill, Sir John Simon, Stanley Baldwin, Lord Birkenhead, Max Beerbohm, G. K. Chesterton, John Sargent, Augustus John, Sinclair Lewis, H. G. Wells, Dean Inge and the Bishop of London.

It was the last, Dr. Winnington-Ingram, who said on one occasion :

" I have not the least hesitation in coming into a tavern, so long as the Press fellows don't dub it as a ' Good pull-up for Bishops.' "

But of all the visitors to the Cheese, none has given it the interest, or been such an asset to it, as Dr. Samuel Johnson, author, wit, philosopher, poet and lexicographer, who lived in and about Fleet Street two hundred years ago. It is a kind of fashion among Fleet Street men to debunk, or try to debunk, the claims of the Cheese to have been a favourite haunt of the burly, gruff-voiced doctor. The usual plaint is that there is no mention of the Cheshire Cheese in Boswell's Life of Johnson ; to which I would reply that Boswell did not become an associate of Dr. Johnson until he was an old man, and had given up his house in

Margot Asquith. June 11th 1898

J. Chamberlain. June 11. 1898

H. H. Asquith. 11 June 98

Mary E. Chamberlain. June 11th 1898

E. Grey. June 11 1898.

R. B. Haldane " "

THEY LUNCHED AT "YE OLDE CHESHIRE CHEESE"

A page from the Visitors' Book showing signatures of Joseph Chamberlain, H. H. Asquith, "Margot," Sir Edward Grey and Mr. Haldane

Gough Square, near the Cheese, as also had Goldsmith, who lived at No. 6, Wine Office Court, opposite the door of the old tavern. But we will return to this.

One thing is certain, that " all the other taverns which Johnson and his disciples frequented have passed away or been improved out of all semblance to the Johnson era ; but the Cheese remains, within and without, the same as it was when Goldsmith reeled up the steps to his lodgings opposite the main entrance in Wine Office Court, or Johnson rolled his huge bulk past it to the house in Gough Square, where the Dictionary was completed in 1755."

I find it impossible to believe that these two fast friends, whose way in and out of Fleet Street lay past the " Cheese," did not make it a regular house of call.

The Mitre, farther up on the opposite side of the Street, is often mentioned as the " real " place which Johnson visited. So it was—when he lived in the Temple, but hardly likely when he lived first in Gough Square, then at Bolt Court, for it is recorded that " nothing short of a hurricane " would tempt the doctor to cross the street.   This is found in a book by one Cyrus Jay, entitled " The Law—What I have Seen, Heard and Known," published in 1868, and dedicated to " The Lawyers and Gentleman with whom I have dined for more than half a century."   Thus :

" During the fifty-five years that I have frequented the Cheshire Cheese Tavern . . . there have been only three landlords. When I first visited the house, I used to meet several very old gentlemen, who remembered Dr. Johnson nightly at the Cheshire Cheese ; and they told me what is not generally known, that the Doctor, whilst living in the Temple, always went to the Mitre or the Essex Head ; but when he removed to Gough Square, and Bolt Court he was a constant visitor to the Cheshire Cheese, because nothing short of a hurricane would have induced him to cross Fleet Street."

Another writer, a Mr. Redding, who himself lived in Gough Square from 1806 onwards, says in his " Fifty Years' Recollections " :

" I have often dined at the Cheshire Cheese. Johnson and his friends, I was informed, used to do the same, and I was told I should see individuals who had met them there. This I found to be correct. The company was more select than in later times.

Johnson had been dead about twenty years, but there were Fleet Street tradesmen who well remembered both Johnson and Goldssmith in this place of entertainment."

I am able to add a further, if somewhat indirect, testimony from a man well known at the Cheese—H. E. Popham, who died as recently as 1944. "Pop," who was on the London end of the *Nottingham Guardian*, had a hobby of writing books about the old inns of London, and I have looked up what he had to say about Dr. Johnson—not without result. He tells of how he had seen a venerable gentleman pottering about the Cheese, and of how, scenting history, he had made the old man's acquaintance.

The age of the ancient one was 90 and his name was Baldwin. He said he had known the Cheese all his life, and Popham led him on to the subject of Johnson, to discover that the old man had met several men in the '60's whose fathers had known the Doctor personally, and had drunk with him at the Cheshire Cheese. This is not exactly conclusive, but " Pop " was a man of great integrity, and, so far as checking historical facts was concerned, of exceptional assiduity. He even made a note of the date of the meeting—November 7th, 1929.

It has been said by detractors of the Johnson tradition that, even if he did use the Cheese, it was but a coffee-house in his time. It has no direct bearing on the question, for the coffeehouses of early days sold liquor as well. In fact, in many of them, the coffee was subsidiary, the owner being at far greater pains to sell his punch than an infusion of the new bean which was just coming into favour.

We may note here that coffee had a pretty poor reception when it was introduced into England in the seventeenth century, as a board in the Rainbow Tavern, opposite Chancery Lane, testifies. The Rainbow was the second oldest coffee-house in London, and was opened by James Farr, a barber, in 1657.

He was not popular with the neighbouring tavern-keepers, who had him indicted as a nuisance in the parish of St. Dunstan's. Thus ran the indictment :

" We present James Farr, barber, for makinge and selling a drink called coffee whereby in makinge same he annoyeth the neighbours by evil smells, and for keeping of Fire for the most part night and day, whereby his chimney and chamber hath been set on Fire, to the great danger and affrightment of his neigh-bours."

But Farr won the day, and so we now have the Rainbow Tavern, rebuilt, but retaining the magnificent Tudor ceiling, a popular haunt of those who make their living by the Law.

If I have made too much of Dr. Johnson, I have done so only in defence of a tradition too often assailed. Let the Cheese have its Johnson, say I.

I wonder how many who speak freely of Johnson, calling him " the great lexicographer," have ever strayed from Boswell to the Dictionary itself. In the Cheshire Cheese is to be seen a first edition of this great work, from which the following extracts are culled :—

Excise.—A hateful tax levied upon commodities and adjudged not by the common judges of property, but wretches hired by those to whom the Excise is paid.

Oats.—A grain which in England is generally given to horses but in Scotland supports the people.

Pie.—Any crust with something in it.

Patron.—Commonly a wretch who supports with insolence and is paid with flattery.

Pension.—An allowance made to anyone without equivalent. In England it is generally understood to mean pay given to a State hireling for treason to his country.

Lexicographer.—A writer of dictionaries. A harmless drudge.

Network.—Anything reticulated or decussated at equal distances, with interstices between the intersections.

How the old boy's chest must have rumbled with mirth as he wrote the last one, and how he must have licked his lips when he wrote the first !

In saying goodbye to the Cheese, we must say it also to the landlord, Jack Bright, as rotund and merry a mine host as you could find in the most ancient of pubs. The accompanying caricature of him is by Sidney Potts, as talented and good-natured an artist as ever blew froth off a Cheshire Cheese tankard.

JACK BRIGHT—HOST OF "YE OLDE CHESHIRE CHEESE"
Caricatured by SIDNEY POTTS

CHAPTER XII

STRANGERS IN " THE STREET "

TOLERANT, wide-hearted and welcoming as its " natives " are, the stranger in Fleet Street is under no illusion as to whether he " belongs " to it or not. I speak mainly, in saying this, of " the places where scribes meet." It is not snobbery. It is simply that the newspaperman, in his off-hours, prefers to talk to men of his own calling, generally about shop.

So-and-so has left the *Mail* and gone to the *Express*, Old *A* has had a row with his Chief Sub. and has been fired. Well, A. is an argumentative cuss, anyhow. B. doesn't seem to get another job, poor devil ; good reporter, too. There's a job going as cartoonist on the N.B.G. The bitter's been awful at " The Angry Rabbit " this week—and so on.

That's how it goes, but don't imagine that it is all small talk. You will find literary and artistic subjects discussed, also general affairs, but always in some indefinable Fleet Street way, which makes an uphill fight of the stranger's effort to join in.

Of course, the stranger's case is somewhat altered if he is the friend of some Fleet Street man ; for then he is more readily accepted, provided he keeps his conversational socks pulled up.

Nevertheless, quite a few strangers have left their mark on Fleet Street's memory, for, in some mysterious way, the Street never fails to attract a miscellany of strange birds which flit about London's social scene. Actors, successful and otherwise, boxers, titled nonentities, crooks, parsons (mainly the wayward ones), jockeys, inventors, bookies, and a host of others, all imbued with the idea that " their lives would make a book," if only someone would write it, descend upon us.

Many of these are quite interesting, and, as you might say, earn their keep. In fact I have made quite a number of friends among this colourful assortment.

One nice fellow whom we were always pleased to see many years ago was a scholarly young chap from Oxford whom I will call Browne, though his name was much more aristocratic than that. At about the middle of each term he used to come to

London for an entirely solitary spree, for he was a valetudinarian, and believed that it was good for his health. He had a perhaps misguided veneration for Fleet Street and never failed to come to it and indulge in the local lotion. He was quiet, he was pale, and he could drink—if only once a term.

Invariably he would land up at Marlborough Street Police Station (or was it Vine Street?), on the insistence of a constable. Then, on the following morning, he would duly appear before the magistrate—generally the same one.

The occasion came when the magistrate decided to give young Mr. Browne a short homily instead of the usual " Pay five shillings," and addressed him somewhat on these lines :—

" This is far from being the first time you have been before me on this disgraceful charge. I should have thought you would have had more respect for your University and, if I am not mistaken " (here he looked over his glasses at Browne's tie), " for the distinguished College to which you belong. Tell me— *why do you do it* ? "

In his high-pitched voice, and with a pained raising of his eyebrows, Browne replied :—

" Purely for valetudinarian reasons."

The magistrate snorted.

" Don't speak to me as though you were the President of the Union," he said.

" But I *am* the President of the Union," answered Browne with an injured shrug.

And he was.

* * *

This was not the only magistrate to be surprised from the dock by a stranger from Fleet Street. There was once an eccentric landscape painter who lived on the coast and made periodical visits to London—and Fleet Street. This always meant an escapade of some kind, out of which the old man always had a joke. On one occasion—and not the first one—he found himself before the Marlborough Street magistrate on the same charge as that which confronted the young valetudinarian. The case was quickly over, and the wayward one was fined a nominal amount which happened to be just half of what he had recently been fined at another court.

" Excuse me, sir—" he began, when he heard the amount.

" What is it ? " asked the magistrate impatiently.

" Well, sir," came the reply, " I thought fines were progressive ; yet you inflict only half of what I was recently fined at your Bow Street branch . . . "

At the use of the word " branch " the whole court tittered, the remaining words being lost as the culprit was ushered out of the dock by an officer.

I once had a grudge against this eccentric artist, though no one could bear him a grudge for long.   I had written a short one-act play to be produced in the programme of a touring party which was playing in the artist's home town.   He had installed himself in the rear of the audience, who knew him as " a character," and I had the mortification of seeing them far more interested in his wise-cracks than they were in my play.

He has now gone to his fathers.   Perhaps I'll try another one-act play one day !

*   *   *

The Venerable Archdeacon Wakeford, of Lincoln Cathedral, was an eminent cleric.   He was also the central figure in the famous Wakeford Case—the " Girl in the Cathedral " case. Later, alas, I knew him as a pathetic " stranger " in the Street of Ink.

I first met the Archdeacon when I was editor of the Northern Newspaper Syndicate in Kendal, mentioned in my first chapter. Looking through my office window one morning I saw a tall, gaitered figure striding down the street.   His shoulders bore the scholar's stoop ; otherwise they might have been those of a wrestler.   Who, I wondered, could this man be ?

I was soon to know, for presently a clerk came to say that Archdeacon Wakeford had called to see the editor.   He had noticed the name-plate outside the offices and, in the impulsive way which I learnt later to be his, decided to make a courtesy call.   Presently he towered into my room, and soon we were chatting about this and that.   It appeared that he had been to Windermere to preach, and was breaking his journey to look around the old town of Kendal.

His face was one of the most powerful I have ever seen.   It seemed to be built of rock.   His eyes pierced one from beneath sandy, bushy eyebrows. Kindly eyes, nevertheless, with a lurking humour about them. So this was the "Venerable John" about whom I had so often read. It needed no undue vision to see him in the pulpit, holding huge congregations enthralled.

We chatted for an hour and he told me he had written a book of "sermonettes" for the lay public. He would be glad if we would undertake to negotiate it for him, which we did. He had already fixed the title : *From Ash Wednesday to Easter Day.*

Poor old Wakeford ! How little did he think that the very next Easter was to mark the beginning of his own Calvary.

For many months after that I had nothing more than a desultory correspondence with him, mainly about his book. Then one morning I opened the newspapers to learn, in a riot of headlines, that he was appearing before the Consistory Court on an immorality charge, to wit, that he had spent a night with a young woman at the "Bull Hotel," Peterborough, during the previous Easter Week. He was denying the charges.

There was much conflicting evidence. Defiantly Wakeford stood there, facing all the heavy artillery of the diocese of Lincoln. The Bishop had fired his heavy guns, and the canons had let off their squibs. The clergy, in fact, were out to have one of their own kind dragged from his office—legitimately, of course.

The hotel register was produced containing the signature of John Wakeford, accompanied, as though as an afterthought, by the words "and wife," written alongside. Wakeford denied that the last two words were written by him. It was too long after the event for hotel servants to be certain of the facts. A distinguished poet, who happened to be staying there at the time, spoke of the Archdeacon breakfasting alone. Some said this ; some that.

A few hours before the alleged night at the "Bull," the Archdeacon was seen walking with a young woman in Peterborough cathedral, a fact which the Archdeacon did not deny. He had gone into the cathedral alone, and had met the girl whom he had shown around the building—and that was all.

It was clear that if he could have produced the young woman to deny that she went with Wakeford to the "Bull," and to prove where she actually had spent the night, the case might have ended differently. But in spite of all appeals, and efforts to trace her, the " Girl in the Cathedral " did not show up. The journal *John Bull* took up the matter, and offered a reward for her appearance, but the girl remained either a mystery or a myth. This action of *John Bull*, incidentally, was after the trial at the Consistory Court, and during the interval between that and Wakeford's appeal to the Privy Council.

The proceedings at the Consistory Court had left the Arch-deacon down but not out. But he was no more fortunate at the Appeal, which was heard by a court of His Majesty's Privy Council, presided over by the Lord Chancellor, Lord Birkenhead. Again it was asked—where was the Girl in the Cathedral ? The end was that the Lord Chancellor delivered a Judgment which will go down in legal history as a masterpiece of prose and logic. But it spelt the doom of the Venerable Archdeacon Wakeford. It spelt the hideous collapse of one of the greatest minds in the Church. It spelt the almost visible disintegration of a noble body. It spelt death.

I should mention that during the case, Wakeford had the support of a large body of public opinion. Proven though the case might have been—and many doubted even that—there was a feeling that the Archdeacon had had a raw deal from the Church. " Alas for the rarity of Christian charity " was the theme of those who saw something revolting in a pack of high-placed clergy relentlessly pursuing one of their brethren.

Soon after the end of this unhappy affair, I came to London to join the firm of Newspaper Features, and it was here that I met John Wakeford again. He had turned to spasmodic journalism, writing articles with all the old spiritual touch which had illumined his sermons in the unreturning years. But he was still seeking the Girl in the Cathedral. Week by week he was finding—or thought he was finding—scraps of evidence which were going to put him right with the world. For had not even the Lord Chancellor of England said that if only he could find the Girl in the Cathedral . . . . ?

It was clear that the light of reason was failing and his frame tiring out. Some time later, we heard that he was in a home. Finally came the news that " the stately column was broke " and that John Wakeford was dead.

A remark he made to me comes often to my mind. We were talking about cathedral cities when he suddenly said : " Shepherd, I will describe a cathedral city for you in one sentence—it is a place where grass grows in the streets and the clergy devour one another."

*   *   *

Frank Austen Smith—whose real name, I think, was Francis Alonzo Smith—was a man of culture, good looks and charm, and, when he died comparatively young a few weeks before my writing this chapter, there were many in Fleet Street who regretted it. His career had been patchy, but any antipathy to this was generally overcome by his charm.

Moreover, there was naturally a deal of sympathy for a man who had stood his trial for alleged murder before the steely and relentless Justice Avory.

I include Frank Smith among Fleet Street strangers, because, when I first knew him, he came into that category. After his trial, he embarked on journalism and worked for some years for *The People*.

Frank's life was colourful from the beginning. He was educated at Eton, after which he spent some years in one of our crack regiments. Afterwards he cracked several fortunes in the true West-End manner. It was after the dissipation of the last of these that he first began to visit Fleet Street on occasions.

No one knew much about him, but we were soon to know plenty, for Frank had a bungalow at Whitstable called *Stella Maris*, and in that bungalow his friend, Jack Derham, was shot dead.

Thus came about the famous *Stella Maris* trial, in which the late Sir Edward Marshall-Hall achieved one of his greatest triumphs. Newspapers had plenty of space then, and scores of columns were devoted daily to the tragedy of *Stella Maris*. It was a case after Fleet Street's own heart. A real *crime passionel*—so it appeared (and I use the last words advisedly). The defence admitted freely that Frank Smith was violently jealous of Derham's attentions to his wife. It was also admitted that Smith had deliberately taken a revolver to *Stella Maris*, where his wife had placed it, during his absence, under a running tap, in the false belief that this would render it ineffective.

Then came a night when the two men had a fierce quarrel at the bungalow. A shot rang out and Derham fell, fatally wounded.

As the facts emerged at the Maidstone Assizes, presented by a skilful prosecution, the chances of an acquittal were generally viewed as slender. The defence was that there had been a struggle during which the shot had been accidentally fired, and that Smith had the revolver with the original intention of shooting himself before the eyes of the man who, he thought, had wronged him.

That was the case as presented with the greatest eloquence by Sir Edward Marshall-Hall. His final address to the jury still holds a high place in forensic records.

But there was a higher one than Marshall-Hall to have the last word with the jury, and that was Mr. Justice Avory, who had already acquired the title of an earlier judge and had come to be known as " The Hanging Judge." This did not mean that he was an unfair judge, for there was none fairer on the Bench. It meant that if a man were guilty, he had an almost negligible chance of sneaking through the net, if Avory were trying the case, no matter how strong his defence, or how eloquent his counsel.

As for his sentences, they were generally as severe as he could make them in the circumstances. When he sentenced Allaway, the murderer of Irene Wilkins, at Winchester Assizes, he sent a cold shiver through all who heard him. After referring to the brutality of the murder, he leaned forward a little and positively hissed the words : "*And you too shall die.*"

On one occasion, he was sentencing a man for a crime which, whether the prisoner knew it or not, could be punished by the " Cat." Avory sentenced him to a spell of penal servitude which, apparently, did not disturb the old lag, who gave the Judge an impudent grin. Avory's small, almost rodent-like face turned even paler than it usually was, and the steely eyes glinted as he added, to the prisoner's horror : " . . . *and* twenty strokes of the Cat " A pretty afterthought.

Such was the man who summed up in the *Stella Maris* case. It was a cold and relentless summing-up which left little doubt in most minds that Avory intended Smith to hang. Then the jury retired.

While they are out, let us take a look at Fleet Street on that Saturday afternoon.

Almost every Sunday newspaper had a splash story about Frank Smith already standing in type, giving all the high-lights of his varied career—School, Army, West End, Whitstable. Some of these bore the signatures of close associates of his, or were prepared from material supplied by them. There had been a brisk, if slightly ghoulish, traffic in this kind of material. I was running a feature agency at the time, which supplied newspapers with every description of feature, sensational and otherwise, and at least three intimates of Smith came to me asking me to negotiate their own story of the man on trial.

I undertook to handle one of them.

Most of these stories were written on the assumption that Smith would be found guilty, and contained a lot of matter which could be published only if their subject was " safely " in the condemned cell. In respect of this, a certain group of Provincial newspapers took a chance, a premature stroke which they later had reason to regret.

On that Saturday afternoon, Fleet Street impatiently awaited the verdict. Avory's summing-up seemed to have put the result beyond all question. The jury were at that very hour discussing whether Frank Austen's future was to be temporal or spiritual. What a time they seemed to be taking over it !

Then the news came. Frank Smith was found Not Guilty of murdering his friend Jack Derham. The charge had not even been reduced to Manslaughter. He was just found Not Guilty. The skill and eloquence of Marshall-Hall had counted with the jury more than had the calculated summing-up of " The Hanging Judge."

There was much scuffling in newspaper offices and most of the " intimate stories," however well-conceived, proved to have been born to blush unseen.

But Frank did not go entirely scot-free. The Judge saw to that. Avory took no pains to conceal his anger at the verdict. Moreover, this was not the first time that Marshall-Hall had beaten him to it. There had been, for instance, a remarkable parallel in the case of the Frenchwoman, Madame Fahmy, who was charged with murdering her Egyptian Prince husband by shooting him in London during a thunderstorm. There was Avory, dispassionate as ever. There also was Marshall-Hall, eloquent as usual. There, too, was the defence that it had been an accident. And there, too, was the jury's verdict of Not Guilty. No, his Lordship was not pleased by the verdict of those Kentish folk at Maidstone.

Here, perhaps, he let his pique over-run itself, for, after the verdict, he waited until Frank was clear of the dock. Then he recalled him and sentenced him to eighteen months for being in illegal possession of a fire-arm—the kind of thing which usually gets a forty-shillings fine.

The next time I met Frank was after his release from prison. I was walking down Fleet Street one morning when I passed a man whose face was grey and whose eyes had a look of fear in them. Not until I had gone some twenty yards did I realise that this was Frank Austen Smith. The lapse of time and the change in his appearance had prevented my recognising him. I turned, hurried after him and shook his hand, congratulating him on his freedom. His blue eyes seemed to grow moist.

" Shep, this is grand," he said. " Various friends have passed me by in London, and quite a few—bless 'em—have spoken to me. But to have a chap *run after me* when he could have dodged me is—well, it's just grand."

I saw quite a lot of Frank after that, for he was frequently in Fleet Street. He talked freely about his ordeal at Maidstone, but there was one aspect of it upon which he absolutely refused to speak. I asked him how he felt and what he thought, while waiting for the jury's return after Avory's summing-up.

" Don't ask me that, old man," he said. " It's the only bit I daren't think about."

I mentioned earlier that a group of Provincial Newspapers went ahead with a story about Smith which would have been better unpublished, for, when Frank heard about it, he at once issued a writ for libel. In fact, he issued writs on each individual newspaper of the group and not on the parent company alone. The result of this was that he was awarded various damages which amounted to a considerable sum. He was in the hands of a very capable lawyer and, between them, they discovered that he had been libelled in several distinct quarters.

For instance, a book had been published, describing a famous murder trial, in which occurred the following :

" Here, not as in the *Stella Maris* case, there was no Marshall-Hall to cheat the gallows of its prey."

How this stupid sentence could have found its way into the book beats me. But there it was, and Smith recovered substantial damages from those responsible. Frank told me that the following piece of argument was suggested by himself to his counsel : What is the prey of a stoat ? Rabbits. What is the prey of an owl ? Mice. What is the prey of a hawk ? Birds. What is the prey of a gallows ? Murderers. Is not the general inference that in all these cases *lawful prey* is indicated ?

The jury thought so, anyway.

Other libel actions followed at intervals and, altogether, Frank must have collected several thousand pounds.

*   *   *

Another stranger in the Street at one time was B. W. Doyle, a genial, bearded figure who had been British Consul in a remote part of West Africa. He liked Fleet Street and was a regular visitor. We on our side liked him, for his stories about West Africa were so descriptive that one could almost imagine having been there oneself. I mention him here partly that I may recount his classic example of the child-like mind of the nigger. He had often mentioned this child-like mind, and one day I asked him to explain, which he did.

At the little residency where he lived, he and his wife employed a native " boy "—a big nigger about twenty-five years old. Doyle was recovering from some tropical illness, and each morning Mrs. Doyle would make him some soup, accompanied by the usual squares of toast. On one occasion she could not be at home to make it so she put the matter in the hands of the boy, telling him to be sure to make the dice of toast.

A long time later she returned to find that Doyle had not yet had his soup, and, going to the kitchen, she found the nigger still busy making the toast. He had first cut the bread into little cubes and was now busy toasting each side of each cube!

*   *   *

There was a period when half the world's newspapers were

daily asking the question " Where is the *Girl Pat* ? " The *Girl Pat* was not a pin-up girl, but a little ship of nineteen tons with a length of 63 feet. Her boss was Skipper Orsborn, with his brother as second in command ; the rest of the crew consisted of four men. The ship left the Humber one day in quite an unauthorised manner on an equally unauthorised voyage, for Dod Orsborn and his brother had decided to have a voyage all to themselves.

Now a ship is not a thing easily missed, and there was a good deal of rumpus about it when she disappeared. There was also a considerable legal rumpus when the brothers Orsborn came back to England at the behest of the authorities, leaving the *Girl Pat* on the other side of the Atlantic.

Dod was in considerable demand by newspapermen, for the story of the *Girl Pat* smacked very much of the days of Drake and Frobisher. That was why Dod Orsborn came to Fleet Street on his return, and gave me the opportunity of meeting him, to find in him an amusing and informative friend. It says much for Dod that, despite his escapade, he became a lieutenant in His Majesty's Navy. I imagine he is just the sort of chap they want.

SKIPPER ORSBORN OF
THE " GIRL PAT "

A one-minute caricature by
Will Farrow

The *Girl Pat* first called at a Spanish port where there was a little trouble with the port authorities and where two of the crew were disembarked. By the time the news of her arrival had reached England, the *Girl Pat*, with her crew of four, was heading into the Atlantic. Where would she turn up next ? That was the question everyone was asking.

For navigation purposes Skipper Orsborn relied on a sixpenny atlas and little else. But he crossed the Atlantic, though it took him sixteen days to do it. One imagines that Sir Francis Drake's spirit looked with approval on that trip of four thousand miles under sail.

Newspapers were still asking the question—" Where is the *Girl Pat* ? "—when Dod had anchored safely at Devil's Island, where he lived for nine days ; then off again into the blue, this time round Cape Finisterre into the Pacific. In all, the *Girl Pat* covered 32,000 miles before she was eventually brought up with a jerk.

The last time I saw Dod Orsborn was early in 1945, when he appeared in Fleet Street in the uniform of a naval lieutenant. To meet the Skipper is to be transported to the great days of Queen Elizabeth. Sincerity, humour, and forthrightness absolutely sparkle from the eyes of this hardy adventurer. Will Farrow, the artist, was with me at our last meeting and did a one-minute sketch of Dod on the back of an envelope. As it is a perfect impression, I reproduce it here exactly as Farrow did it on the spot.

Truly, Fleet Street would not be the place it is, were it not for some of the strangers who come along and adopt us.

CHAPTER XIII

REPORTERS' TALES

I HAVE often heard the question asked—which is the most interesting job in Fleet Street? It is generally conceded that the work of an all-round reporter comes high in the running. He —or she—sees more angles of life than does any other professional person—all facets of human activity—high, low, honest, nefarious, pathetic, humorous and the rest.

Says his News Editor :

" Professor Blink has separated the Jinglebat Streptococcus. Get the story."

" The St. Samuel's maternity home in the East End has just been blitzed. Get a human end to it."

" The Balham murder case comes up to-morrow. Be there. Get a new angle on it."

" The Archbishop is launching a new purity campaign. Find out the details . . ."

" Black Market Inquiry to-day. No, don't go. Get the low-down on the ju-jube racket."

And so on. Thus the reporter ranges over life, his experience of it increasing every day.

Many all-round reporters eventually become specialists—crime specialists, for example. I know several of the latter, and it would be difficult to meet men with more interesting conversation than theirs, once you start them talking about their jobs.

To meet genial Bill Finch, of the Press Association, one would never think that he had covered scores of murder cases and been present at a number of executions. Yet he has. Of all the famous murder cases that Bill Finch, as P.A. Crime Correspondent, has covered in twenty years the one which interested him most was the murder of Elsie Cameron by Norman Thorne at the Chicken Farm at Crowborough.

Bill has been good enough to let me have a first-person account of why the Thorne case ranks as one of the strangest he has covered. Thus he writes :

The Cameron-Thorne case had a fascination that other murder cases lacked. Not only was the evidence of murder purely circumstantial, but the characteristics of the two principals provided interesting psychological reflections.

It was Elsie's determination upon marriage, despite all its manifest drawbacks, that led to the tragedy. Their pre-marital intimacy had disturbed her mind, and being something of a religious neurasthenic, she was convinced that nothing but marriage could right the spiritual wrong.

Thorne was equally determined against it for more material reasons, and his rather crude attempt to dissuade her by suggesting that he had another girl in trouble, only served to impress upon Elsie the need and urgency for a quick marriage. She was impervious to all arguments against marriage. Her unsuitability to be the wife of a struggling poultry farmer because of her delicate physique she swept aside, and the fact that all he had to offer her was a life of poverty in a miserable wooden shed, furnished with a worn-out easy chair, a table and a small wooden chair without a back and a wooden box, was equally ineffective as a deterrent.

It was marriage at all costs for Elsie. Perhaps the medical evidence at the trial that she was " heavily over-sexed " might provide a reasonable explanation.

What happened in the hut when she suddenly turned up to force the marriage, must for ever remain a subject for conjecture.

Her frequently expressed intention to commit suicide if Thorne refused to marry her certainly gave his story—told for the first time at the trial—that she committed suicide a certain amount of credence. He said he found her hanging in the hut and merely cut her down and buried the body, suggesting that she might have attempted to stage a mock suicide to frighten him, but that the " attempt " had proved too realistic.

A plausible theory, but unconvincing so far as the jury were concerned, for they took only thirty minutes to find him guilty of murder.

In Thorne's favour, it must be stated that the medical experts called at the trial disagreed vigorously over the question of whether the mark on Elsie's neck was or was not attributable to hanging.

Before his arrest and trial, he steadfastly denied any knowledge of Elsie's whereabouts, and I remember when Birtenshaw, of the *Evening News*, and myself challenged him on one of our many meetings, he put on a very pained expression at the thought of our disbelieving him. When I asked him : " Now, tell us, where did you bury her body ? " there was a complete *volte face*.

With studied calm he answered : " I buried her underneath the ground where you are standing."

Frankly, both Birtenshaw and I were puzzled at the sudden change of demeanour, and wondered whether he were at last telling the truth.

We communicated our suspicions to Chief Inspector Gillan, of the Yard, and when the farm was dug up, it revealed the fact that he had spoken the truth in every detail.

As I said before, Thorne differed from other murderers I have met. For instance, he was as eager to be questioned by the reporters as they were to question him. Most murderers I have met seek to avoid the Press in the early investigations, being anxious not to be trapped into making any damaging admissions, but Thorne " asked for it," and came almost nightly to the Crest Hotel where we stayed.

His excuse for the visits was his anxiety for news of the woman whose body he had buried. I think he realised we never believed him, but nevertheless he came along each evening to be " grilled."

I have never believed there was anyone who could be definitely classed as the murderer " type," but Norman Thorne was less like a murderer than any other I have met in all my years of crime investigation.

With all his faults, however, one felt he had much good in him. He did not allow the slump that followed the last war to engulf him. As an engineer, he found himself out of work soon after demobilisation, and rather than drift aimlessly about the streets, he began his chicken farm venture, determined that if hard work and perseverance could bring reward, he would achieve it.

After the trial, one had the uneasy feeling that had he used less clumsy methods, not only to disentangle himself from Elsie, daily clamouring for marriage, but in his efforts to conceal her death, he might have " got away " with manslaughter.

Unquestionably, no murder trial in the history of British Justice ever aroused more violent discussions than that of Thorne. The difference of opinion between the two medico-jurists, Spilsbury and Bronte, as to whether the mark on the neck was consistent with hanging or not, was a very memorable feature. Dr. Bronte was convinced it was, and Dr. Spilsbury was equally positive to the contrary.

When the jury returned a verdict of Guilty, Thorne's heavy features paled beneath his shaggy and unkempt hair.

After the trial, Thorne awaited his end with fortitude, and on the day, which, somewhat ironically, would have been the 27th birthday of Elsie Cameron, he was hanged. It was my unpleasant task to attend his execution, and as he came from the condemned cell, I could not help noticing that he winced a little, and that a pallor spread over his face as he saw the grim gallows ahead of him across the intervening corridor. He braced himself in an attempt to walk firmly, but obviously needed the assistance of the two warders who held his arms.

On the scaffold the end was quick. The executioners took him over ; the trap-door was sprung, and the soul of Norman Thorne went to a hell of his own making—or the heaven he professed to anticipate.

The above story is not the only one of its kind which Bill Finch can tell. I knew him for a number of years until the war, when he spent most of his time in what was called the Press Bureau of Scotland Yard. Here he was in touch hourly with everything happening in the world of crime detection. As crime representative of the Press Association, he was an important link between Scotland Yard and the general public. I am sure both are indebted to him.

* * *

How was it, you may ask, that Bill Finch attended at executions ? The reason was, that in at least one county town having a jail, the Sheriff has—or had—the right to admit a newspaperman. An antidote to any suspicion of secrecy.

* * *

Hilde Marchant says later in this chapter that at least forty per cent. of good reporting is good luck. Judging by many of the first-hand stories I have been told, I can well believe it. There is hardly a reporter of note who cannot give examples of stories falling into his hands like the proverbial ripe plum. A particularly good specimen of this was provided me by J. C. Sewell, now leader writer of the *Daily Express*.

Before he took on the task of writing " Opinion " for over three million readers daily—and you may treble that figure if you include non-purchaser readers—Jack Sewell was on the *Daily Telegraph* for fifteen years, during which period he filled almost every job on that paper. He joined it after a distinguished career at Cambridge.

A reporter's life is not spent entirely out of the office. There is often plenty to do, even though there is no immediate outside assignment for him. One summer morning, Jack was running through a newly-published book to see if he could find a story in it, in which case his job would be to follow it up. Suddenly he was called to the news editor, who asked :

" How's your French, Jack ? "

Sewell told him he could speak it quite well.

" Right," said the news editor. " I want you to fly at once to Basle. The Queen of the Belgians has been killed in a motor accident. Car driven by the King left the road and crashed. Get going. We are arranging an hotel for you."

This happened in the office at 12.30. By 1.40 Jack was in a plane bound for Switzerland. The *Daily Telegraph* had their own correspondent in Geneva, but it was thought more expeditious to send Sewell by air than to wait for the Geneva man to reach the scene by car. Of this, the latter was informed.

After landing at Basle, Jack made for Lucerne, which was within easy distance of Küssnacht, where the tragedy had happened. He had scarcely time to look carefully at his hotel, but he concluded that something had gone wrong, for it was a small and rather uninviting place, not quite the kind of hotel the *Daily Telegraph* would reserve for their man. It was called the Hotel Central, and Jack concluded that the office had confused it with the Hotel Continentale, which happened to be the case.

Before long, he was at the spot where the royal car had skidded off the road to end in a wreck down the slope below. By various means, he managed to piece a story together and was back in his hotel, rounding it off prior to 'phoning it to Fleet Street, when a strange thing happened. Through the thin wall partitions of the third-rate hotel, he heard women's voices. Fortunately for Jack they were speaking in French, not German, and he was able to understand. What he heard was something like this :

" And to think Monsieur Schneider was the first to give them help."

" Ah, yes, he was in his car driving behind the King when it happened, but he didn't know it was the King until he found him by the wrecked car."

A moment later Sewell was in the room, telling the women he was an English journalist and asking their help, which they were quite willing to give. Yes, Monsieur Schneider was the chemist at the corner of the street. Yes, one of them would gladly take him round to Schneider's place and introduce him.

Could any reporter wish for better luck than this ? Schneider gave him a first-class story, and by nine o'clock Jack was 'phoning it to his paper. It was a perfect scoop, and the *Daily Telegraph* was the only paper next morning to carry the story.

It happened that Jack Sewell was due for a holiday at that time so, having very naturally taken a liking to the place which harboured Mr. Schneider, he arranged with his paper to start his holiday then and there. He sent for his wife who joined him, and there they spent a happy time, becoming—again quite naturally—friendly with the Mr. Schneider who was responsible for it all.

* * *

Cyril Martin is another newspaperman who has had his share of " scoops from the blue." Slim, sleek and dark, Martin is a first-class reporter on the *Daily Mail* with many strange experiences to his credit.

At one time there was an epidemic of burglaries in big riverside houses from Richmond to Windsor. The police knew that a number of these were the work of one man, but who that man was they could not discover, and, had it not been for Martin's dog, they probably never would have done. Stories of the mystery robberies were appearing in the papers, and the public interest in them was rising. Who was the burglar?

At the time, Cyril Martin was renting a large-sized house on the outskirts of Richmond, and was awakened one night by his dog growling below. Going downstairs, he found the animal sniffing and snarling at the kitchen door, which opened on to the spacious garden. He opened the door quickly and was just in time to see a man disappear at full speed into the darkness of the lawn, obviously, thought Martin, making for some waste land behind it.

It was futile to give chase, so Martin hurried to the telephone and rang the police who, in an amazingly short time, were on the spot. Beginning what they thought would be a long and probably fruitless search, they were astonished to find the man lying prone and dazed on the lawn a little beyond the spot where Martin had seen him disappear. The police promptly took the man in charge and, by some of the valuables found on him, it was easy to deduce that here was the burglar whom the police were seeking from Richmond to Windsor.

What had happened was this. Only that morning Martin had mentioned to his wife that it might be dangerous to leave out the clothes-line at nights, as she was in the habit of doing. Unluckily for the burglar, she had forgotten to act on Martin's advice, with the result that the rope caught him under the chin as he dashed into it and gave him the equivalent to a knock-out blow. He was just recovering when the police arrived.

Unfortunate as it proved to be for the burglar, it was a real stroke of luck for Martin, who was able to 'phone the story to the *Daily Mail* in time to catch their later editions. So the *Mail* was able to give its readers the exclusive story for which they had been waiting.

Telling me of the incident later, Martin invented an amusing American headline for the story : CRIME REPORTER'S WIFE'S WASHING-LINE CATCHES CROOK.

Cases of " mistaken identity " do not, as a rule, act to the mistaken one's advantage, but an exception certainly occurred to Martin when, in his usual capacity of reporter, he was mistaken for something morbidly different. The story is really one of bitter tragedy but, as far as Martin is concerned, it has a definitely humorous angle.

It began with a Society wedding at St. Margaret's Church, Westminster, where one of the bridesmaids was a beautiful girl whose home was in Kent. The service over, the girl declined to go on to the reception ; instead, she entered her chauffeur-driven car and drove back to her Kentish home where, to the horror of all who knew her, and to many who did not, she shot herself.

One supposes, of course, that she was in love with the bridegroom. Be that as it may, it fell to Cyril Martin to go to Kent for the *Daily Mail*, with a photographer, to get the story. The expedition started badly by the pair missing their train at Victoria and having to wait for the next, eventually reaching the nearest station to the girl's country home, only to encounter a bunch of rival reporters on their way back.

" It's no good," said one. " You may as well come back with us. There's a tough butler at the door, and a couple of Alsatians as well, and neither of 'em like reporters. If you come back, we'll give you all the copy we have."

" Thanks very much," replied Martin, " but I may as well take a few pictures of the house now I'm here."

There was a solitary hire-cab in the station yard. Martin and the photographer entered it and asked to be driven to the house. They were dressed, I should mention, in black coats and striped trousers. The photographer had his camera in an attache case ; it looked more harmless that way.

Leaving the cab, they rang a great jangling bell, whereupon the door was opened by the grave-faced, hushed-voiced butler. Martin was ready for the worst, to make a getaway, even, but to his astonishment, he and his colleagues were invited into the hall.

" A very sad affair," said the butler, offering them chairs, " but I suppose you gentlemen are more or less used to this kind of thing."

" To some extent, yes," replied Martin, " but we always feel very sympathetic, naturally."

" Thank you," said the butler ; then, after a little silence, he went on to say how he had been almost a father to the girl, and she a daughter to him. He told of her early life, her interests and amusements, and, in fact, almost everything Martin wanted to know. Then he said :

" Now I expect you would like to come upstairs."

This was a new one on Martin, and he was beginning to stammer a reply when the butler, noticing his hesitation, asked :

" But you *are* the undertaker's gentlemen, aren't you ? "

" I'm afraid we're not," replied Martin, finding courage. " We're from the *Daily Mail*."

With that, the butler nearly threw a fit. He had betrayed confidences. He had disobeyed instructions and had " spoken to reporters." He would lose his promised pension. He was, in his own words, pretty well done for.

But Martin was not long in putting the old fellow at his ease.

" I promise you," he said, " that there will be nothing in the paper to suggest you have spoken to me. Everything I know will have been given to me by one of the wedding guests. See ? "

The butler saw, and thought the gentlemen from the *Daily Mail* would like a glass of sherry. All was well.

On the following day, Martin's paper came out with an exclusive, which goes to show that even missing a train may have its uses.

There was another contributing factor. The butler was actually expecting the undertakers' men at that time. Surely that was luck on a high level.

*   *   *

I recently came upon a forty-year-old book called " How to Succeed as a Journalist," and in it found the following paragraph :

" The lady journalist will, probably before the next decade has run out, apply for and obtain permanent employment on the reporting staff of the morning newspaper, see her initials daily in the reporter's diary, and take her full share of work, whether it be attendance at police court, bankruptcy court, or assizes ; the reporting of speeches at City Council, public meeting or great political demonstration ; the description of wedding, launch or Royal visit ; or the diplomatic quest of special information, and the hunting up of the latest details of tragedy and disaster. If she has any tendency towards hysteria, she may reasonably be excused from chronicling the grim incident of a private execution."

There was nothing wrong with this prophecy. To-day the

woman reporter is an accepted unit of Fleet Street's personnel although she had to break down a good deal of anti-feminist prejudice at the beginning. Some of this was due to an early self-consciousness which seemed to demand flat heels, a guardsman's stride and, not infrequently, a loud voice which was a pain in the head to the average male journalist who, until then, had been calling his trade—and his haunts—his own.

To-day the woman reporter is just a straight, workmanlike person who has a job to do, and does it well. Phyllis Davies, good-natured and cheerfully built, has been on the *Daily Mail* for sixteen years, during which time she has covered stories of every kind. Her career has never lacked interest. She began as a store detective in London, and I can quite believe her when she says that she cried when she had to make her first arrest of a shoplifter. As it happened, the culprit proved to be an old offender, a fact which made Phil less susceptible afterwards.

With Phyllis Davies and Hilde Marchant, I bracket Vivien Batchelor, star reporter of the *Daily Express*. Astonishingly good-looking, and with a great gift for repartee, Vivien is equal to any story which comes her way.

I count Hilde Marchant as the best-known woman journalist. For varied ability, it would be difficult to find an equal of the diminutive Hilde. She has broadcast, she has addressed thousands in Trafalgar Square, and has covered stories of almost every side of human existence. Previously on the *Daily Express*, she became ace reporter of the *Daily Mirror*. Typical of her good nature is the fact that she has written for me the following sketch of her career as a woman journalist. I print it just as it has come to me :

There was snow on the ground, my shoes leaked and the handle of my cardboard suitcase had broken. In one hand was a single third class ticket to London ; in the other I was trying to drag a small but heavy case along to a railway carriage. The point was that the ticket was single. I was at Hull railway station and going to London. I had done it before, but this was the first time I had had no return ticket.

That is the picture of a nineteen-year-old woman journalist leaving the local paper and home to go to Fleet Street and try and make fame, if not a fortune. Whenever I think of it now, it reminds me of a setting for a Victorian novel. I would be disappointed if there had been no snow and if my shoes were not in the last stages of decay—the best pair being, as all provincials know, reserved for Sundays, and neatly packed in the battered case.

For three years I had worked on the *Hull Daily Mail* as women's page editress and reporter. This is the story I always tell the young and enthusiastic girls who come to see me and say they want to be reporters—it terrifies them, and usually makes good £3 10s. a week secretaries out of them.

Our school magazine, the *Boulevardian* of Hull Boulevard Secondary School, had a monthly competition of 5s. for the best essay or piece of writing in the current issue. I won it five times running, and the head mistress thought this monotonous, so she made me the editor of the paper and told me to write anonymously, thereby not qualify for the prize. I edited the magazine for over a year, then it was time to leave school and decide how to earn a living.

There were several ideas—the head mistress thought I would be a good school teacher, my parents thought I should go into an office, and my mathematics master thought I would be a good journalist. I had no ideas on the subject. The mathematics master, being practical, went to the *Hull Daily Mail*, got an interview for me and pushed me through the door. I saw a man known as a chief sub who offered me 8s. a week to work on the switchboard. I told him it would not keep me in silk stockings, and that I needed 10s. Charmed with this argument, he gave me the job. I learned the job in a few hours and, above all, learned how to listen in to calls. That gave me the first clue and excitement on being a reporter.

I always listened in to their calls—even now I remember that their index number was 11 and 12. The conversation was something like this :—

" Give me the Central Police Station."

Call got and given.

Reporter: " Hello, George. Anything doing ?

Policeman: " Only a couple of bums in the dock, Harry."

Reporter: " No murders, no decent people committed suicide ? "

Policeman: " No.   Three tarts from Hessle Road, but nothing doing.   See you in the bar at lunchtime ? "

Reporter: " Yes, see you in the bar, George."

It occurred to my Yorkshire Penny Bank mind that the reporter was being paid £3 10s. for that, and I was getting the odd shillings. The *Hull Daily Mail* became part of the Rothermere group and changed its editor.   W. S. Robinson, the new editor, walked from his office, past the telephone room every day and then to the composing room.   I stopped him one day and said I wanted to be a reporter, so he said I could be his secretary instead.

Then came the six months that I have valued all my life.   After typing his letters, answering the 'phone and ordering cards for his wife's bridge party, W.S. would hand me an empty white sheet of paper, a duplicate of the feature page of the *Hull Mail,* and ask me how I would fill it, heads, type, pictures, make-up and copy and all, all except the happy holes already filled with advertisements for liver pills or the smoothest matt powder ever invented to entice an unsuspecting young man.

He did, in fact, teach me my trade.   He taught me to go in and feel type, to know type, to know how a page was built and constructed by slow and cynical men known as " comps," who don't care a rap for the written word unless it is in lead.

For three years I edited and wrote the Women's Page, going out on occasional news stories, and generally doing every job on the paper from cattle shows to courts.   W.S. made me learn shorthand, made me study the mysteries of the technical side of the job, because he said writing was not enough ; any young woman from a good school would be just as good at essays as I was. Few would know how to convert this into being a reporter, with a news sense and a sense of the difficulties and technical limitations of a daily newspaper.

He gave me a respect for my job.   So when the enthusiastic and charming young girls ask me how to get a job on a newspaper, I tell them to go to the local newspaper office, persuade them to engage her at any job, then start snooping around and studying the anatomy of newspaper production.

For W. S. Robinson was of the old school of editors.   Man or woman who aspired to join his staff on the editorial side had to have a healthy respect and knowledge of the trade they were going to practise.

When I left and decided to go to Fleet Street and try to crash the national newspaper field, he made a presentation to me, a second-hand typewriter, bought out of the donations given as a farewell present. He said then that I was making a great mistake, and that he would welcome me back on the staff in three months, because I was not really good enough for London.

He was right. Fleet Street was cold and hostile, and I was not good enough. I free-lanced on the border line of starvation for a year. News editors and women's page editresses were kind and offered me my return fare back to the local paper where I belonged.

But by writing five shilling paragraphs for women's pages on the new glass-ware for the table, or the right temperature of baby's bath, I managed to survive. Then finally, after a long struggle, I was taken on the staff of the *Daily Sketch*, because they found I was making too much money as a free lance.

Then the happy days began. Properly trained, beaten and hammered by space work, I was at last ready to begin as a reporter.

I have always disliked this business of " women " reporters. The sex should not matter. I have seen pretty girls enter a reporters' room as new reporters, engaged because of the length of their eyelashes or the swing of their skirts—after all, news editors, despite their reputation, are human. They do not last. Cochran has a place for them, Fleet Street has not.

But no woman survives in Fleet Street unless she has friends. I have had good and real friends, for it is essentially a friendly place.

I remember going on one story, a rather difficult and delicate one, and one which I have forgotten now, but which gave me one of my closest real friends, Margaret Lane. I arrived as usual, hatless, gloveless, stockings slightly twisted, but a good fur coat to hide it all. Margaret was waiting in the office car. She saw me dejected, forlorn, cold, hungry, tired ; in fact, the way most reporters are on a difficult story. We sat in the car nibbling chocolate, finally got our story, went to her home, and I telephoned my office and had a bath, a good dinner, a warm fire, and life flowed just as our warmth and friendship began on that first meeting to flow. Since Margaret Lane left Fleet Street to write books, there has never been a woman reporter with quite her descriptive style, quite her flair for personal interviews.

I was destined always to be found in this forlorn state by Margaret. There was the case of the Abdication. I had kept guard on Mrs. Simpson's house in Regent's Park for twelve hours before I learned she had left for France. Then at midnight the *Express*—I had transferred to them—got Lord Beaverbrook's private plane and flew me over to Paris. Then began one of those absurd but essential chases that newspapers and their reporters indulge in. I followed Mrs. Simpson by car all across France to the Riviera. It was a dreary journey, and I had no luggage, no hat—just a handbag to clutch, with the usual expenses of £100. . . wealthy but uncared for.

When I arrived at Cannes, at seven in the morning, dirty and sleepless, there was a message waiting for me : " Arriving on Blue Train 8.30 Book rooms. Love Margaret."

I had time only for coffee, then met the train with the grime and filth of two days in my hair, hands and face. Margaret stepped off the train, immaculate, followed by four small suitcases, all neatly covered and bound in linen.

We booked the biggest suite in the Grand Hotel, Cannes, we shared stockings, she took me out to buy a hat and some clean underwear, then we started on the story. I learned one golden rule on that occasion—comfort leads to good reporting. It is a legend, dying hard, that reporters must look like tramps and be alcoholics in order to be good.

I have found in my years in Fleet Street that journalism has taught me to love the human race. We usually visit people when some drama has made their drab daily lives of sufficient interest to be termed news. We see them when they have won the Irish Sweep, have married their housekeeper, murdered their grandmother, given birth to more than the normal quota of children, have grown the largest onion on earth or have crashed on the Stock Exchange. We see the human race at war, we attend its birth, its marriage, and slowly walk, with notebook in hand, at its funeral, carefully taking the initials of the mourners. But as a reporter who has had tea with a murderess, refusing sugar because she was addicted to dropping arsenic in the sugar bowl, and taking tea with a fisherman's wife who had just lost her entire family of husband and three sons in a lifeboat tragedy, my appetite for soaking up the details of the human scene is inexhaustible. If it went, and I became detached and cynical, I know I would be a bad reporter. Tears must fall when a house, and the neat, tight little families within it, are blown to dust, or the reporter is ceasing to reflect the emotion of the people reading the story in the morning.

I have had a lot of fun in Fleet Street of a buccaneering kind. One night I was peacefully cooking my dinner when the foreign editor 'phoned and said I was to fly to Paris and pick up the exclusive story of a woman who had shot her husband. She had been aquitted on compassionate grounds by a French court in the South of France. She was an Englishwoman and she had blown off the top of her husband's head when he had provoked her beyond endurance. The French take a sympathetic view of such things.

I met the woman in Paris as she came off the Blue Train and we drove around the city and saw the sights, then started back for England. She was a homely, pleasant type of woman, a typical English provincial housewife who had had her troubles. We discussed the tragedy in a private room on the cross-Channel boat—me flat on my back because the sea was mountain high and it was the roughest crossing I can ever remember. Feeling ill but being devoted to duty, I gradually had the whole sordid story out of her, when she felt the authenticity of her case must be proved. She pulled out a white handkerchief, and said that if I didn't believe her, here was proof. In the handkerchief was the shrivelled top of her husband's skull. She intended to keep it in loving memory.

There are other occasions. One night I was told that I would have to be in Warsaw the following evening at eight o'clock, air passage booked, nothing to worry about. I pointed out that it was necessary to have three visas for such a trip—one through France, one into Germany and one into Poland, but this was waved aside as one of those technicalities which a little pressure and ingenuity rapidly overcame. All was well until the last stage of the journey—from Berlin to Warsaw. The plane was of the old, string-bound type being used by Polish airways, and it was attempting to fly through a snow storm, at the height of about a hundred feet, or so it seemed. In front of me was a priest who obviously saw the end, and was counting his beads and reciting the burial service in Latin. The other passenger was a Polish business man who insisted on smoking a foul cigar and tapping the ash on the petrol tanks.

On such occasions, one says farewell to life and recollects how good it has been. We arrived in Warsaw and I was met by a representative of the Polish Foreign Office. But our correspondent was not there. He sat in a car, and I wondered why until we arrived at his office and he was carried out, lowered on to a small cart and propelled himself to his office. He was one of the most brilliant correspondents, but he had no legs. He did it all by telephone.

I love flying, but sometimes the situation is rather disturbing ; for example, the time I flew to Spain to report the Spanish war and my companion was a communist organiser, a woman. We had to fly over the Pyrenees in an electric storm and we were bouncing around like feathers in a gale. She seemed to think this a suitable occasion to recall the intimate and surgical details of a particularly unpleasant operation she had just had in France.

Sometimes a story rests entirely on your own ingenuity and luck—at least forty per cent. of all good reporting is good luck. I was stranded in Marseilles trying to reach Spain for the final collapse of the war. I went for a swim. I had tried but failed to get boat passage. It was impossible. But watching a swimmer come out of a dive, I saw my old friend " Potato " Jones. He was running the blockade again, and I could go on the ship as a deck hand. I bought a pair of dungarees and we were ready to sail, but it was too late. The Spanish war was over.

It took me several weeks to convince the editor of the *Express* that there was a job of work for a woman reporter to do at war. Many of us have had similar struggles, the perpetual battle against what I call the pots, pans, hems and tucks of journalism.

It was the news editor's idea that the woman reporter, attached to the staff more as a novelty than a workman, should go out and find what colour lipstick women were going to use this year, whether navy blue eyelashes would ever be a fashion, or if high skirts and red petticoats were to be worn. It changed when news editors found that the women on the staff could look up railway trains, go to a story and sweat in a telephone box, putting it over with the same vigour and interest as the men on the staff. It changed when they found that women readers were just as interested in news as the men who wrote such indignant letters to the papers—women readers being too busy in their homes to write.

When I first joined the *Express*, I found I had to go on a diet—a wearisome, monotonous business in Fleet Street when steak and kidney pudding was a real dish. I found I had to have my hair sheared by razors and cut in a certain topsy fashion to prove something, that I had to go to Halifax and be used as bait along the dark and narrow streets for a slasher supposed to be abroad. This latter idea also occurred to the news editor of the *Daily Mail*.

One dark and slightly foggy night in Halifax, two women reporters were crawling around the dimly lighted alley-ways of that city, scared out of their wits, enticing a slasher to pounce out of the shadowy loneliness of those streets. It was Phyllis Davies, of the *Daily Mail*, and myself. We had both been assigned this unwholesome job of testing the statements of many good, sound North countrywomen that there was a man in their district pouncing out with an open razor.

Next morning, Phyllis and I had rival but equally brave stories of our midnight crawls. My greatest fear had been going down a side alley in the pitch darkness, waiting to be slashed, and catching my face in a strong, firm spider's web. I was too scared to shout to the photographer waiting at the end of the close to take the photograph. I hesitated a few seconds, then, trembling and shivering, caught hold of the spider's web and found it was a clothes-line strung across the narrow alley.

Phyllis Davies and I are friends, and always will be when we meet on stories. This does not mean we share our stories. Far from it. Phil is too good a workman to seek help from anyone. She goes about her job like the confident, trained and experienced reporter she is. No detail, no dreary dragging around the police station and streets ever stops her tracking to the last comma the story she had come out to write.

We have met many times, but the last and best was when

we found ourselves side by side in the first, select batch of British women war correspondents being released on Europe.

There had been a long and tough struggle with the War Office to get British accredited women war correspondents somewhere near the war front. In all this, Phil Davies, of the *Mail*, and myself were the hardest fighters. For Phil and I had seen something in Fleet Street we had hoped never to see—women reporters accredited to the American army preceding us by months ; not a scoop, but a privilege of being attached to the U.S. forces instead of the B.L.A. We saw brigadiers, we argued, we finally had our uniforms and six British women went over to Paris. Phil was next to me in the plane, and we believed we were going off to war to do a job of work in our own newspapers for the British army.

We were dropped in Paris and told to stay, and were handed a sheaf of invitations to fashion shows which we both ceremoniously dropped in the waste paper basket. We fidgeted around Paris until one morning both of us were missing. Phil had gone on a long front line journey with French women welfare workers, I was travelling in a jeep, inches deep in water and in blinding rain, going towards the British Second Army. Eventually the authorities caught up with us, but we had both been somewhere near the British fighting soldier, and when we were finally thrown out of Paris, we had the satisfaction of having seen our own countrymen in action, and the satisfaction of getting our newspapers to publish our stories.

It is ironic, but having been able to cover two of Europe's wars—the Spanish revolution and the Russo-Finnish war—I found it a hard struggle to report our own serving and fighting men in the line.

But the privileges won from news editors—that is, the right to sit at a murder trial or go to a war—have been too hard earned by the tradition of women journalists in Fleet Street to be stolen from us lightly by the War Office.

There is much to remember, with humour and satisfaction, in my Fleet Street days. I remember the day when I was at the famous Ruxton murder trial, and had bought an air cushion because the benches in the court were narrow and hard. In the middle of a grim part of evidence, the valve in the cushion jumped out, and there was a heavy and noisy sigh through the court. There was the time when I was spending my nights among the East Enders in the blitz and started a campaign to improve their shelters. It succeeded. Living among those people in the moments of acute danger and watching death sweep, like the very fires that were started, through the streets of simple working people, was perhaps the greatest experience Fleet Street gave me. For those days and nights in the East End, at Warden's Post 11, with the firemen, with the ambulance drivers, showing only a Press card to enter the greatest story I have ever seen, I am deeply grateful. It gave me more than words—it made me a citizen of London.

CHAPTER XIV

PRINTERS' PIE

IT sometimes happens in a printing works that an assembly of type, in single metal lines or letters, gets upset, the result being a mixture of type of no particular order. This is known as " Printers' Pie." Hence this chapter, which contains a miscellany of matter.

One of the most amusing men to work in Fleet Street was C. W. Miles—to some, Charlie ; to others, Billy. He was a newspaperman with a kindly disposition, a lively if slightly acid sense of humour, a red nose and a Welsh accent. I imagine there were more good stories told about Billy Miles than any other man I have known. Humour clung to him alike in prosperity and adversity, and, owing to precarious health, he had his share of the latter. He has died since this book was started, and often made fun of himself when he felt that he had but a little time to live.

At times one could have imagined that the Witch of Fleet Street had singled him out for special sport, as I am sure she did when he obtained the job of publicity man for a steamship company. He was to go on a long tour in a brand new ship, a tour which was to take him to the Pacific coast of America. It was a first-rate job, to be paid for mainly by a lump sum on his return, his duties being to prepare articles for subsequent publication in the world's Press, and to get publicity matter into newspapers published at different ports of call.

All this went well.

Not unexpectedly, however, there occurred on the boat several mishaps inseparable from a first major voyage. In one case, something went wrong with a piston, and the ship's engineers, with great ingenuity, remedied the matter by means of a piece of steel which they cut out of the deck. It was really a little triumph in its way.

In similar difficulties, the engineers surmounted them without the passengers even knowing. But Billy Miles knew about them and made notes, for here, surely, was good publicity for a shipping line so well equipped with inventive engineers.

On the boat's return to Britain, a call was made in the Thames before the voyage was terminated at the home port of Cardiff. Miles, eager to start his publicity, decided to remain in London over the following week-end, go by train to Cardiff and rejoin the ship there, or at least meet her skipper in the head offices of the Company, which were in Cardiff.

Accordingly, Miles wrote his story about the inventive engineers and took it to the *Sunday Dispatch*, who agreed to publish it. But the bright boys on that paper saw a better angle to the story than that of inventive engineers. They gave it headlines which almost suggested the voyage had been calamitous—quite an excusable way of looking at the story as given to them by Miles. The paper went even further and sent local contents bills to Cardiff calling attention to it.

Next week, Miles turned up at Cardiff, and the first thing he saw on emerging from the station were Sunday's bills carrying the words " CARDIFF HOODOO SHIP." Miles paled, for to call a ship " hoodoo " might well deter another crew sailing in her, because sailors are notoriously superstitious. Further, this was not the kind of " publicity " which the Company expected from their own man !

Miles made his way to the ship, fearing the worst. He did not fear in vain, for he was met by an enraged skipper who practically forbade him to come aboard. He then went to the Company's offices, hoping against hope that he would be given his money, which was a considerable sum. Here, again, he was refused audience.

There was nothing for it but to return to London, where he went to see the *Sunday Dispatch*. They, quite rightly, failed to see where, in the circumstances, they had been at fault, for Miles had not told them that the story was meant to be publicity for the Line. He was, however, given work to do on the paper, which was some compensation, but whether he ever received his money from the steamship company, I never learnt.

Yet Billy Miles never told this story without all the humorous embellishments of which he was capable.

Then the Witch of Fleet Street had another " go " at him. It was really unfair in this case, for Miles was suffering from an affection of the eyes which necessitated his wearing bandages, and seeing only with difficulty. Altogether, Billy had come up against an unusually lean patch.

Lord Camrose, now owner of the *Daily Telegraph*, was then Sir William Berry, and himself a Welshman. Miles had known him in the past, perhaps in their native Wales, and thought a meeting with the kindly Sir William might possibly lead to a job. Accordingly he rang up Sir William's London office, and asked his secretary if she could arrange an interview.

" I'm sorry," she said, " but Sir William is engaged this afternoon, and he is leaving for South Wales by the first train in the morning from Paddington. Perhaps if you approached him on the platform, he could spare you a few minutes."

Miles always said he had known Sir William Berry well enough to call him Bill, so the possibilities for the morning seemed promising.

He awoke in his room in old Clifford's Inn, to find the morning foggy, and, worse still, that by some mischance he had only threepence in his pocket. Still, by bus plus walking, he could reach Paddington with a penny left wherewith to buy a platform ticket. Owing to the fog and the state of his eyes, he ran his timing rather close, but managed to flounder into the station.

More or less groping, he found the slot machine and inserted the penny which he had reserved for his platform ticket. But the old Witch was on his tracks by this time, and, when he pulled the handle, out came a wafer of milk chocolate. He had gone to the wrong machine! He had not another penny, and the time for Sir William's departure was approaching. Perhaps, even now, he was already in a compartment, unfindable.

Miles made his way to the barrier and showed the ticket collector his chocolate, laughing as he explained. The collector laughed also. This was good—a chap trying to get on the platform with a bit of milk chocolate, and the more Miles tried to explain, the more the man laughed.

In fact, he laughed until Sir William's train slid out of the station. No doubt the Witch laughed, too. So, eventually did Miles.

Despite his natural Welsh accent, Billy was one of the best Cockney impersonators I have known, and he had a wide repertoire of songs and recitations, many of them his own compositions. One of his most successful efforts was " The Dock-yarders' Children," a slightly cynical eight-liner inspired during the great unemployment period. It went to the tune of " Just Like the Ivy." Thus :

> " The dockyarders' children,
> A-sittin' on the dockyard wall,
> Watching their fahvers
> Doing —— all.
>
> And as they grows older
> They'll be dockyarders, too.
> Just like their fahvers
> —— all to do."

I have seen Billy Miles hold the Press Club bar for an hour with similar efforts, never being allowed to stop without giving his classic recitation, " The Moslim," in perfect Cockney :

> " Oh, the Moslim looked dahn on his prisinger,
> A-lying upon the grahnd.
> The prisinger was bleeding pro-foosly,
> His blood it was dyeing the sand.
>
> Oh, the Moslim looked dahn on his prisinger,
> *Then*—frowing away his gun,
> Said ' I don't fink I can
> Kill this poor bleedin' man.
>
> (And here Miles reverently raised hat.)
> *He must be some pore mother's son.'* "

These verses, cold as they may seem on the printed page, became classics on the lips of Billy Miles.

* * *

Sir Charles Higham might have been called the pioneer of modern advertising. He certainly brought new methods into the practice of it, and showed a somewhat startled advertising world how to do it in The Big Way. He saw beyond the advertising of branded goods, and was largely instrumental for introducing a more embracing form of publicity. Thus, while various advertising agents were pushing this and that particular brand, Sir Charles was becoming busy on a campaign to make people eat more bread of any kind. He acted for the Millers' Association, to whom the consumption of flour in any form was important.

Starting his Press and poster campaign with the slogan "Eat More Bread," he soon changed it to "Bread for Energy," a phrase soon known throughout the land. It was at this period that I first became acquainted with him. I heard that he was on the look-out for editorial articles emphasising the value of bread in diet, and, as a number of feature articles were passing through my hands at the time, I went to see him with one or two ideas.

To meet Sir Charles Higham for the first time was an experience, for, apart from being an expert at advertising other people's goods, he was a genius at advertising himself. His extensive offices were in Kingsway, and there were few callers who were not impressed by the enormous white Rolls-Royce standing outside. Short of having two of them, an Indian rajah could not have done better.

Sir Charles' own room was a revelation. It was panelled entirely with what appeared to be cedar-wood. The furnishing was most sparse. Indeed, the only thing I seemed to see when I entered was a desk with Sir Charles sitting behind it, looking rather like the last cigar in a box.

I am sorry to have to speak of Sir Charles in the past tense, for he was one of the most likeable Big Noises I ever met. He had a gay habit of making one feel at home from the start, and, whilst he was a good talker, I think he liked listening better, provided you had something to say. The words "well-groomed" and "well-preserved" applied to him in equal measure. Perhaps his face was slightly fleshy, but his crisp, rippling hair, iron-grey, made you forget that.

Soon we came to an arrangement whereby I should supply

him with pro-bread articles by doctors, scientists, sportsmen and others. Then, one spring morning, he said :

" Wouldn't it be great if we could persuade the Oxford and Cambridge crews to say they are training on bread ? But, of course, it's impossible."

" I'll try, if you like," I said. " What's it worth ? "

He mentioned a sum, and I returned to my office to think it over. There was no time to lose, for Boat Race Day was not far ahead. It was impossible for me to go to the crews' respective training quarters, and it was certainly not a matter which could be done by correspondence. Then I thought of a press agent named G. B. Clements, a newcomer to Fleet Street, whom I knew well as a free-lance publicity man. I also knew him as a man who never took No for an answer.

Clements was as keen as I thought he would be, and next morning set off in his car to the Cambridge training quarters. That afternoon I had a telegram from him : " Have fixed Cambridge Going to See Oxford." Sure enough he came to me on the following day to say that all was well, with the exception that the crews would only sign to the effect that they trained, not on bread, but on toast. If this were all right, then the President of each crew would " sign on the dotted line."

I rang up Sir Charles to ask if it were all right, and he said that toast would meet the case. He was rather sceptical about it coming off even then, but, of course, he didn't know Clements ! He then made a condition which I thought would kill the idea—that he would write the " copy " on his own copy-paper, and that it would be necessary for each President to sign respectively.

The " copy " from Sir Charles was fortunately dignified and restrained. Nevertheless, Clements was a little dubious as he set off in his car again. Two more telegrams reached me that day saying that the necessary signatures had been obtained, and I rang up Sir Charles to tell him the good news. He was over-joyed.

" Why, the Millers' Association bet me we wouldn't do it, and I've won my bet ! " he said. " Well done ! "

Boat Race Saturday came on the heels of this episode, and I eagerly scanned the Sunday papers to see how Sir Charles had presented the world with the fact that the Oxford and Cambridge crews had trained on bread—or rather, toast. I might have known ! Only one crew appeared in his advertisement, and that was the winner. He had made arrangements all round so that whichever crew won—well—they had trained on Bread—For Energy !

A pretty stroke, as they say on the river.

It was G. B. Clements who pulled off one of the most outstanding publicity efforts in quite a different direction. A woman named Miles, of St. Neot's, gave birth to quadruplets, and no sooner did Clements read the news than he was in his car, heading for St. Neot's as fast as he could. This, of course, is nothing to a reporter, but Clements was not a reporter. He was a publicity man. Without much persuasion, he obtained the signatures of the parents to an agreement whereby he should handle all the publicity about the St. Neot's Quads, as they soon became known.

For a brief period, Clements was on tenterhooks (whatever *they* are) lest one of the Quads should die ; but they all survived, and he found himself master of the situation as far as news, photographs and advertising value went. You would read a story of the daily life of these mites. It came *via* Clements. You saw a photograph of the four of them in their bath. It came from Clements, and it was he who fixed up contracts with baby-food makers and others, all willing to pay well for the privilege and publicity of supplying the Quads. Anniversaries offered plenty of scope, and newspapers fell over each other to secure pictures of them at their first birthday party, just as they did when the first Quad was able to walk.

I have no idea of the total revenue " earned " by this famous little litter, but it must have run into many thousands of pounds. The handling of the matter, however, was not without its anxieties to Clements, for he had to contend with a host of Fleet Street reporters and camera men, many of whom were always on the look-out for chances to get stories and pictures behind his back. Had they known Clem better, they wouldn't have tried.

*   *   *

It was at about this time that Darts were emerging from the four-ale bar to find favour in Mayfair and even in Buckingham Palace itself. Soon almost everyone was playing this " working man's game." It invaded clubs of all kinds from St. James's to Stepney, and no road-house dared be without its darts board. As a player of long-standing, and not a bad one, either, I was naturally much interested to see this grub evolving as a butterfly. I began to visit darts tournaments and to write articles on the game in general. They were not difficult to sell, for editors were fully alive to the hold which the game was acquiring. Even *Punch* had picture-jokes about it, one of which was particularly good. It showed a little Cockney with cap and muffler, carrying a little bag, at the imposing door of a Mayfair mansion. A pompous footman was looking down upon him doubtingly. " 'S all right," the little man was saying, " I've come to give the guv'nor his darts lessons."

Apart from articles in periodicals, I soon found myself writing darts notes several times weekly in the *Star*, and darts news every Sunday in the *People* and the *Referee*. All this meant that I had to keep contact with various darts leagues, such as that of the Licensed Victuallers and the Theatre Darts League, and it was through such activities that I made the acquaintance of Seagers, the gin people. They were beginning to take an interest in the game. It was a smart move, for, with women taking up the game in their thousands, it was going to mean a great increase in the consumption of gin-and-lime. What better, therefore, than that Seager's Gin should be associated with darts ?

To further this, they had fitted up a large darts " parlour " in a building by the Chelsea Embankment. It was beautifully done, the walls being decorated by a comic " history of darts " painted in life size by one of the famous Zinkheisen sisters. I gave some assistance to their publicity man, Major O'Beirne, and this led to my being asked to organise a Press team to play against a Theatre team. Gordon Harker, by the way, was president of the Theatre Darts League at the time.

I had almost completed my team of well-known literary men, when Seager's managing director went to America, and the event had to be postponed until his return—by which time the darts season was over. After that, sterner things intervened in Europe and the postponement continued. It had been Seagers' intention to have Stanley Holloway in their team, and I produced a recitation for him to give on the occasion, based on his famous character,

Sam Small. I doubt, however, if it ever reached Stanley, owing to the circumstances I have mentioned. I print the verses here, pointing out to non-players that a " ton " is a score of 100 and that " double one " is regarded as the most difficult number on the board.

> " Sam Small he were a working man.
> To rise in life were Sam Small's plan ;
> He played darts well, and double ones
> Came easy to him, so did " tons."
> But this is what kept Sam Small down—
> He only played at t'Rose and Crown.
> And Darts, of course, as we all know,
> Has ceased to be a game that's low.
>
> As time went on, Sam's game bucked oop ;
> He won the local Brewery Cup,
> And this as you may rightly guess,
> Got him into t'local Press.
> London papers followed suit,
> And one, than all the rest more cute,
> The very moment that they read it,
> Begged Sam their Darts Page to edit.
>
> Sam played in clubs now, not in pubs,
> With Editors and toffs, not Subs.
> One day he played Lord Rothermere
> (Fizz on t'game, of course, not beer).
> Each wanted double one to win,
> And Sam! He goes and throws it in!
> His Lordship gave Sam one fierce frown,
> And now Sam's back at t'Rose and Crown."

I imagine this would have gone down well at the Press *v*. Stage match.

* * *

It was in the course of writing about darts that I once walked into Claridge's, that home of Ambassadors, and asked the magnificent hall-porter where the dart board was located.

" The *what* ? " he queried, without undue politeness.

" The dart board," I repeated. " My friend and I thought we'd like a game."

" Dart board—in *Claridge's!* " he managed to say. " You must be mistaken."

" Not at all," I replied. " I know there's one in the place somewhere."

He motioned to another stalwart, who came and towered above us. Did we think Claridge's was a pub, or what?

I was repeating my request when a sort of manager came up to see what was going on. He, of course, was most emphatic about there being no dart board in Claridge's. In fact, he rather intimated that the conversation was at an end.

" Very well," I said, " will you please direct me to the Balkan Fair, which I understand is being held here? "

" Er—certainly," he said. " I'll show you, but——"

Presently we arrived at a room where a section of the Fair was being held and there, as I knew it would be, was a dart board on the wall.

" Thank you," I said. " I knew you had a dart board somewhere in the place."

But the manager had gone.

I am not sure that the occasion was a Balkan Fair, but it was something of the sort, organised by the Posh for the Posh in aid of some worthy object.

Peter Burnup, film critic and newspaperman, also has a Posh Hotel incident to his credit. It began, I think, with his disapproval of the Press arrangements at some function given in the hotel. Anyhow, Peter and pals turned up at the P.H. one night, and, seating themselves at a table, they asked in the politest manner if they might see the manager. They required some information from him, they said, and, when that functionary arrived, Peter looked up at him blandly and asked :

" Excuse me, sir, but could you tell us if this is a Watney house? "

★   ★   ★

John o' London's Weekly is a literary journal which seems to have established itself as an institution on its own. Those who know it are not all familiar with the fact that John o' London was a real person. He was Wilfred Whitten, who was, I think, the first man to use that pseudonym. He was one of the last of the scholars, as such, in Fleet Street, where, for a good half century, he took his wine and talked books with any kindred spirit he might find. I am glad to have known him in his last years.

How eagerly some of us used to wait on certain days in El Vino for the appearance of old Wilfred, with his apple cheeks and white hair. He was a testy old boy, nevertheless, and you had to make but a mild literary *faux pas* to get a cracking " Don't be stupid " from the lips of John o' London.

Despite the disparity in our ages, he and I struck up a friendship, sustained though it was by short meetings only. Our chief pleasure lay in putting up some old literary problem and each trying to solve it by the time we next met. Not that you could call this one exactly literary : I asked him one day what was the origin of the phrase often encountered in the country—" As tight as a fiddler's bitch."

We formed a few theories, one of mine being that it went back to the days when the fiddler and his wife tramped the countryside, the former playing his fiddle at harvest homes, country dances and the like, while the latter stayed in the inn to finish up " under the weather."

But by the next meeting, Wilfred had ferreted out the real origin, which was : " As tight as a fiddle's bridge."

We also found out that the phrase " don't care a tinker's damn " has nothing to do with swearing, but that the word " dam " is correct, referring to the little wad of clay, thrown away after it had served the tinker's purpose by damming a hole in a pan which was being soldered. We became rather tangled about all this, for the phrase " don't care a curse (or cuss) " called for explanation. Was there any connection between not caring a curse and not caring a damn ?

But Wilfred had it solved by our next meeting, having discovered that the Old English for a blade of grass was *kers*, so that the phrase was really : " don't care a *kers* " which, of course, is the same as not caring a straw. This also explained a phrase I had picked up in Shropshire : " I don't care a curse off a common." It means, of course, that one doesn't care a *kers*, or blade of grass, off the whole of a common.

In the same way, Wilfred maintained that if a countryman said " I axed him if he'd seen a wopse " he was really using the Old English words *aeks* and *waeps*.

Of course, these explanations stand to be challenged, but they, and others like them. gave John o' London and myself a considerable amount of fun.

James Dunn (R. E. Corder) would sometimes be with us. On one occasion, Jimmy had just come back from Dublin and was full of a newly discovered Irish poet, a tram conductor or something, who had become a sensation in Dublin literary circles. Ireland had only recently produced such playwrights as Sean O'Casey and Liam O'Flaherty, and now, said Dunn, she had given the literary world a new poet in this genius called Higgins.

" He's not known in England yet," said Jimmy to Whitten, " so you've got a great chance to introduce him through *John o' London's Weekly*. A literary scoop, Wilfred."

But Whitten said nothing. He appeared to be deep in thought.

" Come on, Wilfred," pressed Dunn. " He's a wonderful find, and Dublin's mad about him. What do you think about it ? "

Then Wilfred spoke.

" Well, I'll tell you," he said. " I think it's a pity his name's Higgins."

Jimmy Dunn gave it up after that.

Nevertheless, Higgins became a poet of importance, both in Dublin and beyond.

*　　　*　　　*

Dublin was an early and particular love of mine when I was philandering with most of the cities in the British Isles. As I mentioned earlier, it was at one time my job to make frequent visits to editors of papers great and small, discussing with them such features as serial stories, articles, short stories and weekly columns which were supplied by the feature agency with which I was connected. I found in Dublin a newspaper fellowship which I have experienced nowhere outside Fleet Street itself. Despite the trouble which was brewing between the two countries —and I visited Dublin both before and during the rebellion—an Englishman unconnected with anything Governmental could always be sure of friendly treatment. When that Englishman was

a journalist, on a visit to the Dublin newspapers, the word
" friendly " became a poor expression, and the newspapermen of
the city set out to give him a really good time.

A more go-as-you-please lot than those newspapermen I never
met, before a tightening-up process began some years later. I
often wondered how some of the newspapers ever came out on
time, with their staffs in and out of Keogh's Bar and the Oval in
Middle Abbey Street all day long. There seemed to be an
understood *laissez-faire* attitude to work ; yet the papers *did*
come out on time, and none the worse for it, either. So casual
were some of the men there, that I sometimes sped over to Dublin
to get a reply to a letter, as being the quickest way in the end.

I occasionally made a trip, lasting but a few days, which involved calling on editors in Edinburgh, Glasgow, Belfast and
Dublin. This meant travelling by night as much as possible, and
one evening found me in Glasgow, anxious to go across to Belfast
with the least delay. I could have made it *via* Stranraer, or
possibly Ayr, and asked advice from G. C. Porteous, editor of the
Glasgow Weekly Herald. Of course, if I *wanted* a train journey,
he said, I could have it, but why not board a boat in the heart of
Glasgow and make one job of it ? Then I learnt that a boat was
leaving Broomielaws quay that night for Belfast. I have been
grateful to Porteous ever since, for he started me on a trip which
I shall always remember.

There were not many passengers, and, as the sailing hour
was late, most of them went straight to their bunks, so that I
was almost alone on deck as the boat slid quietly down the Clyde
in the moonlight. On either bank, in the great yards, loomed
ships in all stages of construction, some of them noble, completed
hulks, others like ghostly skeletons in the silvery light. Here
and there, as we moved towards Greenock, were furnaces belching
flames, whose reflections tinged the Clyde with orange light. No
wonder I stayed there until we were heading for the open sea !

When I descended to the saloon I found one solitary passenger,
a tall, good-looking chap, having a final drink with the steward.
He asked me to join him, which I did, little thinking that it would
mean more than saying good-night. Actually it led to an
adventure in Dublin on the following night which might have
meant that I should never see the Clyde again.

I learned that his name was Mac, that he was a D.I.—a District Inspector in the Irish Constabulary—and that he was returning from some months' recuperation after having been left for dead in a ditch by the Sinn Feiners. Dublin knew stirring times in those days.

Mac and I stayed up much of the night, and it was arranged that he should leave me to see my editors in Belfast, and follow him to Dublin later in the day, which I did. He had not to report at Dublin Castle until the following day, so he suggested that he should stay at my hotel—the Royal Hibernian. As he was as fond of whisky as any man I have met, it was with trepidation that I joined him in the evening. Although a Scot, he had a perfect Irish accent, acquired during many years in the country, and he was quite at home in the company of Sinn Feiners, whom we met in the various resorts to which he took me.

Later, when I began to speak of going to bed, he cheerfully said that the evening was only just beginning. The next thing was that I found myself on a side-car—to Englishmen a jaunting car—on the way to a place which he said was called Grady's Club. Our driver's horse knew his job, and streaked through the streets of Dublin as though he were racing at the Curragh. These " jaunting cars," by the way, make a precarious perch for the unpractised.

And so we came to " the club," which appeared to be several slummy dwellings converted into one. A strange scene met my eyes. The big room was dimly lit, and in the middle of it was a large table at the head of which sat Grady himself, dispensing porter from a huge jug at a shilling a glass. Middle-aged and ample, he was undoubtedly king of the proceedings, and his order for less noise, given in a concentrated brogue, was obeyed by the motley crew who sat round the table or on chairs elsewhere in the room. One sensed the place to be frequented by the more fanatical of the Sinn Feiners of both sexes. Only a Hogarth could have done justice to that picture.

I was mystified—and still am—about a girl I found in a corner of that drab room. She was dressed in a black silk frock and lay on a bed which in the circumstances seemed strangely white. There were other rooms and beds upstairs, but this girl did not belong to them.

Presently I went to the bedside and spoke to her. She lifted her heavy lids and raised her blonde head a little as though to take stock of her surroundings. Then she muttered, " Oh, my head," and apparently went to sleep. No one took any notice of her, which was strange, for her lithe, black figure lying on the white sheet was surely nothing ordinary. I went over and asked Mac if he could explain it, but he could not. He just told me to keep away unless I were looking for trouble, which, at that moment, he happened to be doing himself.

A girl, a Sinn Feiner, had been shot dead that morning on College Green in Dublin, but no one knew who had shot her. The murder was attributed, of course, and probably rightly, to the Black-and-Tans, many of whom at that period were scarcely fair specimens of young Englishmen. Or the killer might have been one of the native rival factions in the city. No one knew, but had they done so, there would have been desperate doings in Dublin that night. It was not without alarm, therefore, that I heard Mac, now in his cups, saying loudly in his Irish accent :

" And supposing I told ye that *I* was the man who shot her. What would ye do about it ? "

I was scared they might discover that he was not an Irishman at all, but one of the hated District Inspectors ; but the fact that he was " oiled " saved the situation. Beyond a few curious looks being directed at him, nothing happened. Meanwhile, the girl in black lay motionless. Something made me wonder if there were not some link-up between her and the girl who had met her death that morning on College Green. Hostages were not unknown in those days.

I managed to make Mac cease his bravado, and eventually we reached our hotel without anything untoward happening. I recounted the story next day to an Irish editor, who said I had probably been very lucky, for more than one man had gone to that club, not to be seen again until his body was found in the nearby Liffey.

*   *   *

Macdonald Hastings is a young man of many parts. Son of the famous playwright, the late Basil Macdonald Hastings, he is an elegant writer, an excellent broadcaster and a first-class shot.

He is connected with the Edward Hulton organisation, and his work is frequently to be seen in *Lilliput* and the brilliant *Picture Post*. Some years ago I met the tall, bespectacled Mac, and he told me he was raising money for some particularly deserving cause. He had hit upon a new idea, which was to obtain as gifts, first editions of books by famous living writers, then to send the books to their authors to be autographed which, of course, would enhance the value of the volumes.

In this way he came to send a first edition of Max Beerbohm to the " incomparable Max " himself. Max, it is hardly necessary to remind the reader, is a brother of the late Sir Herbert Beerbohm Tree, and, as Sir Max, is now one of the few examples of Edwardian literary and artistic genius—a delicate essayist, a penetrating caricaturist.

It needed the whimsical mind of Max Beerbohm to spot that the publishers' imprint had an iambic ring about it. An *Iambus*, for those who don't know, is a poetical foot containing two syllables, with the accent on the second. You have it, for instance, all through Gray's Elegy, thus : " The *cur*/few *tolls*/the *knell*/of *part*/ing *day*." Max saw that (" rightly read," as he says), the imprint might carry the Iambic form :

> London : John *Lane*, The *Bod*ley *Head*
> New *York* : Charles *Scrib*ner's *Sons*

so he wrote beneath it :

> This bald announcement, rightly read,
> Iambically runs.

*   *   *

We now take you over to the studio ; in other words, we will take a look at the B.B.C. in its more apparent relationship with Fleet Street. It is no secret that the newspapers have suffered a good deal of heartburnings because of big news being released through the B.B.C. at some tantalising hour ; which means that by the time the paper prints it, it is stale, or at least has lost its kick.

Otherwise the relations between Broadcasting House and Fleet Street are cordial. So they should be, for the B.B.C. owes a great deal to Fleet Street. This applies particularly to the Monitoring Service, which has been called the " Third Ear of Great Britain "; it is an organisation which listens in to every foreign broadcast, and eventually produces a printed and bound summary of the millions of words heard daily from foreign countries.

This summary is called the " Daily Digest of World Broadcasts." It sometimes contains as many as 100,000 words of the previous day's broadcasts, and is ready by 10.30 each morning for collection and distribution in official circles. Let me quote from an American source a flattering reference to the British Monitoring Service, made in an article on America's own inception of a similar service during the war.

" There is another listening post system along the lines of which America may pattern its own. Somewhere in the English countryside is the ' Third Ear of Great Britain,' as it is called. Everything on the English air comes in for its share of examination by the Third Ear.

" At present more than 230 broadcasts in thirty languages from more than forty countries are monitored, recorded, translated, summarised, edited and distributed daily by the B.B.C. Third Ear experts to all the Ministries of State engaged in the prosecution of the war.

" The process is complicated, but it flows with the smoothness of a stream. It begins at dozens of aerials at various places remote from cities, where signals from transmitters ranging from Lwow in the Ukraine to Rio de Janeiro in Brazil are intercepted. The signals, through headphones, stimulate the ears of half a hundred polyglot monitoring listeners gathered from the four corners of the world.

" This remarkable body of men was assembled, member by member, with the utmost care. Of necessity, each person must be trustworthy, and each must be intimately acquainted with the affairs and customs of a country being watched for evidences of propaganda. In the English system, a million or more words are transcribed daily. Recording machines are set in motion when a button is pressed. From it all, daily reports are compiled.

" So the process goes on, endlessly, somewhere in the heart of the English countryside."

The English countryside! I know that bit of it, and have many a time been jostled in the streets of an old-fashioned town by Indians, Brazilians, Turks and I don't know what besides, each of them doing his vital job at the Monitoring Service. In due time it will no doubt be told how this quiet countryside community became a veritable town of Babel, with its population trebled, as it were, overnight. It may also be told how the Monitoring personnel put up with accommodation which, by circumstances, could be nothing but uncomfortable.

An important part of the Monitoring Service is the Editorial Unit, whose job it is to cope journalistically with the vast amount of material which ultimately appears in the Daily Digest. This is a job which calls for Fleet Street skill and gets it, for you may number by the dozen the familiar Fleet Street men making the best of their self-imposed exile. They are men accustomed to working in a hurry, to handling news with the speed and confidence only to be found in a newspaper office.

Nor is the Monitoring Service the only B.B.C. section of which Fleet Street men form an integral part. Thus I could mention a dozen newspapermen on whom the Overseas Service is partly dependent. At least six of them are ex-*Daily Telegraph* men, while two of them are from the Press Association.

No, the B.B.C. is not entirely run by its own young men!

Even a number of its regular features are akin to journalism. What was " In Town To-night," for instance, but straight reporting, interviewing? Indeed, J. C. Cannell, who, with Eric Maschwitz, was partly responsible for its inception, was a Fleet Street journalist before he turned to radio. He was actually responsible for bringing several thousand people of all kinds to the microphone. He knew the right way to approach them and get the best out of them. It was no new job to him.

Cannell has many good stories to tell of his adventures and contretemps in securing subjects for " In Town To-night "; in fact, he has written a book about them.

Discussing animal stories with him one day, he went back to the days when J. C. Stobart, the great educational authority, the man who invented " The Grand Good-night," brought to the B.B.C. a canary which he alleged would sing according to orders.

Stobart's standing was so high that anything he said went.

So the canary was introduced to the B.B.C.—the famous singing canary.

These were the days when for the first time the nightingale had been heard on the air ; these were the days when men hid in bushes to try to catch the notes of this elusive bird ; then came Stobart with a ready-made feathered songster !

So the canary, with all its certificates, so to speak, was given special privileges on the understanding that he would sing on the Tuesday. He had already given evidence that he was the genuine sing-to-order canary, and all seemed well. In the canteen they put him in a special cage, a gilded cage. A man was assigned to look after him . . . special seed was bought . . . he became, indeed, a gilded bird.

Then came the Tuesday. A smooth-voiced announcer said, " We have here a canary that will sing to order—sing, indeed, at request. Listen . . . "

But would that bird sing ?

Not a note. Thus he joined the parrot who refused to talk, the singing mouse which refused to make a sound, and the Fleet Street dog who refused to bark. No, the B.B.C. have not been happy in bringing animals to the mike. They should start a Dumb Friends' League of their own.

* * *

Homogeneous as journalism may be, many newspapermen become specialists and rarely work outside their own adopted branch. For instance, there is William Barkley, whose rare touch enlivens the Parliamentary news in the *Daily Express*. Bill practically lives at the House of Commons. Then there are such men as Ian Mackay, of the *News-Chronicle*, and Trevor Evans, of the *Daily Express*, who have Britain's industrial set-up, politically and otherwise, at their finger-tips. Then there are the agricultural correspondents, like Kenneth Pipe, who, in the *Express*, regularly interprets English agriculture to the public, especially as it concerns food.

Another specialist is Harold Watkins, of *Cavalcade*, who also writes on radio matters for the Kemsley group of newspapers— an interesting job, and one which brings him into contact with all the personalities of the radio world.

Then there are sports journalists, who have a field of their own.

Nor must we overlook those reporters who specialise in their expenses sheets !

An unusual specialist is Louis P. Snelgrove. His line is puzzles, particularly the crossword variety. In an earlier chapter I have described how I was instrumental in launching Crosswords in Britain through the *Sunday Express*. At that time, I was prepared to believe that I had introduced merely a craze of the moment, yet to-day, twenty years afterwards, there is scarcely a Fleet Street newspaper without its Crossword puzzle. A development which I was far from foreseeing was the competition value which the Crossword attained. Soon newspapers were offering large money prizes for solutions of their puzzles. The interest in these puzzles may be judged by the fact that to give, say, a prize of £500, a paper must receive 20,000 sixpences from competitors, without allowing for expenses and scrutiny staff. Assuming that the papers probably make a large profit as well, one can imagine the enormous numbers of entries sent in.

The path of cash Crosswords promoters has not been smooth, for various lawsuits had to be fought as to whether the puzzle was a matter of skill or luck. The late Lord Hewart, when Lord Chief Justice, laid down that such puzzles were legally valid when they demanded a preponderance of skill, which seems a somewhat elastic ruling. Luck can take strange forms, an unsuspected one being luck in using the right dictionary. It has been known for a newspaper, though saying that any word may be found in a certain standard dictionary, not to specify which edition of that dictionary may contain it. Thus a competitor may be *un*lucky in not having the right edition, the edition which alone contains the word pre-adjudicated as the right one.

Louis Snelgrove has made the Crossword his especial study, and, apart from compiling them, has won numerous prizes, large and small ; and well he might, for he has mastered every intricacy, every compiler's device and, in fact, every trick of the game. At one time, and in various ways, Snelgrove was making several thousand pounds a year from puzzles.

Newspapers certainly have reason to respect the smiling, slightly sandy Louis, for his interest in Crosswords even runs to keeping records of published clues, a practice which once enabled him to make a paper pay out its prize money twice over.

The paper had published a Crossword in which a word might have been *A*bcd or *Z*bcd. The correct solution, or, rather, the one decided by the paper to be the right one, was *A*bcd. But the ever-watchful Louis turned up his records and discovered that the paper had used the same clue in a puzzle some months earlier, when the correct solution was stated to be *Z*bcd. It was obvious that those competitors who, on the second occasion, had sent in *Z* were as much entitled to their share of prize-money as those who had sent in A. Convinced of the fairness of this, Louis tackled the paper, with the result I have mentioned above. But I don't think the paper liked him for it, all the same !

On the whole, however, newspaper Crossword puzzles are ably conducted and fairly run.

Another competition specialist is Edward Johnstone. Most people in Fleet Street know Johnnie, but ask any of them for which paper he writes and one will mention a " Sunday," another a daily, and yet another a sports weekly. Few know that at least a dozen pen-names mean Edward Johnstone.

Slouching along among his friends, this pale-faced chap, whose clothes are usually as powdered with cigarette-ash as former denizens of the Street were dappled with snuff, is reticent about his being such a specialist.

Some thirteen years ago he tackled Crosswords from a different angle to that of Louis Snelgrove ; he set himself to conquer the mathematical problems involved in combining alternative solutions. As " Mathesis " in the defunct *Guide for Competitors* he built up a circle of followers and later convinced the *Racing and Football Outlook* that his methods could be used successfully in football pools. He became " Mathematician " on that paper with remarkable results, continued up to date.

He is also "Jack Boulder" (John Stone!) of the *Sunday Dispatch* in which paper he recently pointed out that a man who had just won £3,000 for a single column in a certain column pool on his coupon might, without winning, have submitted $1\frac{1}{2}$ million different combinations of the results concerned. Johnnie knows these things.

Incidentally, he is publicity man for I.T.P. and Western Pools, and is generally the last court of appeal on any matter of permutations and combinations. From all of which, you will gather, he makes a lot of money. His wife, Eileen, whom Fleet Street rarely sees, but likes when it does, is his collaborator in the various pools tables in newspapers and the books of which he has a number to his credit.

*   *   *

The part played by journalists in the late war has been considerable, and one of which the public is little aware. It knows, of course, about war correspondents, many of whom have lost their lives—I believe over forty English-speaking correspondents have been killed—but it little appreciates the work Fleet Street men have done in less conspicuous fields.

Thus the now disbanded Ministry of Information owed much to newspapermen who, at no great rates of pay, gave for years their experience in news handling to that one-time cumbersome machine. It was not easy work, for the layman, briefed in a little authority, often proved obstructive.

The News Division of the Ministry owed much of its smooth working to Ronnie Church, its Assistant Director, who came from Fleet Street to oil the wheels, and oiled them well. It would be difficult to say which is the most outstanding feature of the shortish, humorous-minded Church, iron-grey and shock-headed—his unobtrusive energy or his understanding of men.

In the vast Press Room, too, you could find many Fleet Street men, each representing a newspaper, and each, generally, with his own telephone box. Their job was to await information from the authorities, pick out the story and 'phone it through direct to their respective newspapers.

In the many recent war areas, wherever troops' newspapers are still being produced, there you will find journalists bringing out, under difficult conditions, lively newspapers for the men.

Not the least of the services which Fleet Street has rendered to the country was its " supply " of Public Relations Officers to the various Ministries. Part of their duties was to answer queries, at all times of the day or night, from newspapers requiring information on some specific point.

" Is it correct that a shipment of bananas is expected in the country very soon ? " asks the *Daily Something*. Jimmy Sinclair, of the Food Ministry, would have the answer. Queries also came in from lesser journals, some of them so stupid that Jimmy would not have been surprised to be asked if pig is pork.

Indeed, stupid questions were a minor bane of the P.R.O.'s life. William Blackley, now of the *News of the World*, spent several years as a Public Relations Officer at the War Office, and has plenty of good stories to tell. These are a few of the queries which came to Bill :

From a reporter : " Could we have details of the time and place of the next Commando raid on the Continent ? "

From another : " Is it true that young officers are being conducted round slaughter-houses to accustom them to the sight of blood ? "

In the case of another reporter seeking a story, Bill told him to see a certain officer at an address at Shepherd's Bush, from whom he would obtain all the information he wanted. Blackley was exceedingly busy at the time, and one can imagine his feelings when, five minutes later, the reporter rang again to ask which was the best way to go to Shepherd's Bush.

I need hardly say that these inquiries came not from old hands, but from boy reporters whom staff shortage had imposed on Fleet Street.

On one occasion, at least, Bill must have relished replying to a query. When the big sweep-back from Egypt was at its height, an angry mother telephoned to say that her son had been called up although he had only one eye, and what was the War Office going to do about it ?

Bill is not unknown to have a sardonic look now and then, and I imagine it came out in full on that occasion as he replied :

" Well, General Wavell has only one eye ; so what ? "

*　　　*　　　*

It is customary with a book of this kind for the author to write some sort of sentimental epilogue. Not so in this case. The book just ends. I was never much of a hand at tying up parcels.

THE END

INDEX